# SHOCKPROOF

## How to Hardwire Your Business for Lasting Success

### DEBRA JACOBS
### GARRETT SHERIDAN
### JUAN PABLO GONZÁLEZ

WILEY

John Wiley & Sons, Inc.

For general information on our other products and services or for technical support, please contact our Customer Care Department within the United States at (800) 762-2974, outside the United States at (317) 572-3993 or fax (317) 572-4002.

Wiley also publishes its books in a variety of electronic formats. Some content that appears in print may not be available in electronic books. For more information about Wiley products, visit our web site at www.wiley.com.

ISBN 978-0-470-87254-3 (cloth)

ISBN 978-0-470-93974-1 (ebk)

ISBN 978-0-470-95003-6 (ebk)

ISBN 978-0-470-93975-8 (ebk)

Printed in the United States of America

10 9 8 7 6 5 4 3 2 1

# CONTENTS

# FOREWORD

In today's business world, shocks are common. Whether the shock is the price of oil spiking to $147 per barrel, a sudden global financial crisis, or a new and disruptive technology, business leaders must prepare for the unexpected or run the risk of becoming obsolete. Of course, it's difficult to be prepared for the unknown. There are so many future scenarios, it is possible for leaders to get lost in "what if?" and lose sight of where they are headed. At Qualcomm, we have worked hard to create a culture that fosters resilience and adaptability. I believe this culture has been instrumental in helping us innovate, overcome obstacles, and capitalize on world-changing opportunities. These themes are at the core of *Shockproof: How to Hardwire Your Business for Lasting Success*.

*Shockproof* tells the story of leaders who align business strategy, organization, and talent to achieve and bolster business results. This alignment does not have to start in the C-suite or be assigned to a project leader. Rather, any leader can use an understanding of *Shockproofing* to more readily accomplish desired outcomes. This book illustrates that better businesses are more likely to emerge when priorities, work processes, and the critical skills of people are continually recalibrated, as conditions change. It is my belief that leaders in any sized organization and industry can benefit from asking themselves two simple questions. (1) How Shockproof is our business, *really*? (2) What can we do today to improve the alignment between what needs to be done, how we are organized to do the work, and the way we engage people to get the job done?

—Dr. Paul Jacobs,
Chairman and CEO, Qualcomm Incorporated

# *A Shockproof Future*

It's the year 2015. You're sneaking a quick peek at the cover article in the current *Fortune* magazine using the latest generation of iPad interactive technology. The article's headline is simple and compelling:

> The Verdict Is In: The Most Successful
> Global Businesses Are Shockproof

As your eyes scan the iPad screen, the narrative scrolls or stops as you ponder new phrases or skip across familiar terms. The images automatically resize as you need them, the 3-D photos appearing in the tablet's new holographic display.

The story behind the headline greatly interests you. For months you have been hearing about the remarkable successes of so-called Shockproof companies where leaders dynamically align business strategy, organization design, talent, and management practices to achieve admirable results.

The article showcases dozens of successful businesses that began the quest right around 2010 to develop the habits of a Shockproof enterprise. The results are eye-popping, and the iPad graphics fire your imagination. As you read, you learn that the recession that crippled the global economy beginning in 2008 helped spur numerous leaders to take bold steps to ensure their workplaces would never again be so unprepared to adapt to changing business conditions, whatever the magnitude.

With one move of the eye you extract a chart that summarizes the results achieved by these featured businesses: Some of the names are familiar household names; others are brand new. Almost every industry is represented. You ponder, what made them capable of accomplishing astonishing achievements in the midst of economic, social, and political adversity?

You realize that a number of these businesses have performed so well that many of their competitors are now out of business or facing bankruptcy. You are eager to dive in and find out more about the choices they made that helped them to so nimbly execute their business strategies and adapt and respond to challenges and opportunities.

A few more blinks of the eye and you find within the article another reference to the Shockproof approach and read that these companies shared a common belief that they had the potential to develop ". . . the inherent capability of evolving to overcome challenges and capitalize on emerging opportunities."

During the last few years, several studies were conducted to determine which factors were most frequently associated with organizational agility and adaptability, and the results became further evidence that a relentless focus on the connections between strategy, organization, and talent provide a clear competitive advantage in unlocking value. You use an app that compares research findings and it spits out four themes common to all the research cited in the *Fortune* article.

1. Everyone in the business is in sync with and laser-focused on the same high-priority goals that create value for the business.

2. The business is organized to be the right size and shape so that everyone is able to efficiently and effectively achieve shared goals.

3. People have the right skills and necessary attributes to do the work they have been selected to do.

4. Leaders continually adjust how the business is designed and talent is managed so that both align with changes in strategy.

You wonder whether a discipline as straightforward and pragmatic as this Shockproof approach could actually be the key to execution issues associated with your global business.

Farther down you read that, "Business strategists and leadership experts first coined the term *Shockproof* in 2008 and it inaugurated an earnest dialogue with leaders about how to intentionally develop the capacity to become a Shockproof enterprise."

Looking up from the tablet you suddenly remember a strategy execution course sponsored by your alma mater; you and your project team did research on emerging thinking in the area of strategy execution. You also recall a group of straight-talking management consultants who were researching and writing about the relationship between strategy alignment and strategy execution. They shared new ideas about the kind of thinking that helps leaders, anywhere in the organization, better connect strategy, organization, and talent to achieve results. You had meant to read their book, *Shockproof: How to Hardwire Your Business for Lasting Success*, but the day-to-day grind, putting out fires, and hitting quarterly goals took priority, and you never took the time to do so.

You decide now to shut down the *Fortune* article and move to the Kindle icon on the iPad. It's time.

You download the latest edition of *Shockproof* and start reading. . . .

# CHAPTER 1

## *Beware the Big Blue Catfish*

We will now discuss in a little more
detail the Struggle for Existence.
—Charles Darwin

As a business leader you enjoy connecting the dots between your own experience and new ideas. That's how you've always learned. Reading about Shockproof businesses and their successes has gotten you fired up. You begin to think about the last time you had a chance to step back from the daily grind and get a fresh perspective. It was at a conference in New York several years ago; where investment bankers and C-suite executives spoke in mostly Darwinian terms about winning and what it takes to compete. You remember an especially entertaining speaker talking about a predatory, big blue catfish that had wiped out several other species of fish with the relentless focus of a trained assassin. The same charismatic speaker referenced celebrity chef Mario Batali, who regularly quips about humans sitting atop the food chain. He'll put it this way, the speaker quipped, pointing at a PowerPoint picture of a chef inspecting a table of unsuspecting diners: *If you're slower than me, dumber than me, and you taste good . . . pass the salt!*[1]

He also presented a video clip of the African savannah, featuring a kudu running for its life, having been cut out of the herd by a pride of lions. The speaker's style was polished and his delivery was engaging, but it was the wide array of stories and examples related to his claims about the natural world that most captured your attention. The message and the intended "takeaway" was clear: "It's good to be the king!"

The next speaker used different analogies, but the message was basically the same: Everybody wants to win and be the top dog, or lead lion, or big blue catfish—pick your species—but the message is the same. It's even woven into our popular culture. The song "Only the Strong Survive"[2] has been recorded three times since 1969. The songwriter and Darwin seem to agree that certain species have the ability to adapt, survive, and flourish in the face of long odds, whereas others don't. Size doesn't always matter. T-rex only comes to life in fantasies like *Night at the Museum and Jurassic Park*; but those pesky cockroaches? They've been around for quite a while, and it doesn't look like they're going away anytime soon.

Of course, while you might have a boss whose management style resembles that of a T-rex, and a few annoying, insectlike associates, the blinding flash of the obvious is that the corporate world hotly embraces the concept of survival of the fittest. Take it to the bank. Corporate board rooms, blogs, and conference calls echo daily with various versions of Mario the predator or the big blue catfish or the kudu on the run. *Kill or be killed, eat or be eaten, grow or die* are clichés, for sure, but they get lots of airtime.

Once you hit the airline lounge at LaGuardia on your way home from the conference, you found a moment to think. Over meticulously sliced pieces of cheese and a glass of wine, you began to reflect on what you heard. You realized, even then, that your company's strategy was not centered around an *eat or be eaten* growth mentality. For years your CEO had emphasized your company's high level of customer focus as its "special sauce"—irresistible, and the envy of your competitors. This level of customer intimacy is not a "bigger is better strategy"; rather, it is about your business developing its own winning game and sticking to it, without becoming distracted or derailed by the aggressive tactics of others.

There is something you read about the teaser on "Being Shockproof" in *Fortune* that recalls the sentiment you experienced in the airline lounge three years ago. A core principle is the belief that every business needs to find its own "best game" and stick to that game, learn to play it better than anyone else, and focus on improving personal best, versus beating the competition at their game. You know you have little personal interest in you or your business turning into "a big blue catfish." You always liked the idea of your company providing something of unique value, versus being "too big to fail." After all, so much of your company's success has been achieved through unique products and services that are hard to mimic, along with a hardwired respect for cooperation and collaboration with your suppliers and customers. Kudus and catfish? Hmmm . . .

There is a very clear and intriguing contrast between the ideas you remember from the conference and the type of thinking that initially got you enthused when you read the *Shockproof* summary.

You fire up your iPad, call up that *Fortune* article, and hit the next Learn More link under Shockproof. "That's more like it," you whisper under your breath, looking for a comfortable spot to settle in and get to the goods. You have often wondered how *Good to Great*[3] profiled companies, which not too long ago were high flyers and front runners, ended up losing their edge and fell to the back of the pack, or went out of business altogether.

Conversely, you wonder, why are some companies simply more resilient than others? Some businesses that you would have bet against surviving, or assumed would be gobbled up, are still standing. Whether it was cunning or strength or just plain hard work, companies like IBM have somehow survived and thrived, and a revitalized Apple is prospering, with new product launches and stock at all time highs. Jerry Butler wasn't writing about corporate America when he penned "Only the Strong Survive," but as an anthem for the businesses that remain high performers in the face of economic, social, and political challenges, it is a highly appropriate sentiment. After all, you don't want to be the one glimpsing Mario over your shoulder with the salt shaker. Yet, you believe that acquisitive growth for the sake of size is outdated. There must be more; a different way.

You hit the Collapse Themes icon after touching all three of the articles that popped up earlier, and discover a few interesting similarities among them. These are summarized in a text table that shows up in the hologram feature of your device.

Businesses that stay the course stand out because their leaders are hardwired to pay attention to critical connections between their strategy, how their organizations are designed, and how they manage talent. These businesses demonstrate a sixth sense that makes it possible to see what their competitors cannot when it comes to interpreting market trends and customer needs, product innovation, process improvement, and defining the skills needed in the future. Just as important, these businesses can "take a hit" and bounce back from situations where a product or an idea falls short of their original expectations, or when a competitor temporarily leap-frogs their capabilities, products, or service offerings. Simply put, they rebound in response to challenges, and they are agile enough to adjust and capitalize on new opportunities.

You highlight the Definition tab on your reader to get the most recent definition of *Shockproof* to show up on the Web:

- Agile, and can quickly reprioritize goals and objectives as business conditions change.

- Led by leaders who understand how to mobilize people and deliver results.

- Highly flexible structures and practices that ensure the right people are doing the right work at the right time.

- Staffed with a workforce that is adaptive and inherently motivated because they are performing work that is directly connected to the business strategy.

- Defined by people who are energized by change and the rewards of success.

Reading on, you discover that not all Shockproof companies demonstrate each of these characteristics in equal measure. In some cases, they might have developed the traits organically over the years. Some companies exhibit the traits because their leaders have been paying close attention to value creation and have adopted over the years sound leadership practices and operating principles that are now firmly embedded in their companies' cultures. In other cases, through pure trial and error, business leaders may have stumbled on the key to becoming Shockproof. But when capability is combined with the intention to focus on these characteristics, it is rare that the results are anything less than potent and sustainable.

Like a race car driver at the front of the pack, who suddenly spins out, only to regain traction and go on to win the race by a large margin, a successful company might lose its way, then regain its sense of direction and go on to be more successful than ever. In some circumstances, businesses that always seem to "qualify to start at the post" continually refine their performance through the efforts of not just talented "drivers of value," but their proverbial "pit crews" who are able to somehow carve away extra seconds of time to propel the business to Victory Lane. And like the race team who can never seem to put their driver into a position to win, or rarely qualify for a race, we've watched as companies continued to stumble, never to regain their balance. We've also seen companies breathe the rarified air of success, only to abruptly hit the wall and spiral right out of business.

Shockproof companies are more resilient and successful for a reason: They get the connections right between strategy, organization, and talent, and calibrate them effectively in response to changing business conditions. Then, like the synchronized cylinders in the winning race car pumping with energy and power, and a team with a singular focus, they figure out how to stay ahead of the field. When they encounter a challenge, they adjust and overcome. When they encounter an opportunity, they are quick to change course and pursue it with impressive focus and discipline. These companies may also lose a few races; but when they do, they learn. They learn what kind of fine-tuning is necessary to their strategy, their organization design, or their approach to managing talent. They learn how to make calibrations or adjustments along the way, dynamically and in real time. Seeing what adjustments need to take place, and understanding how to make these calibrations, is the work of leaders. When leaders act to align strategy, organization, and talent, their businesses get better at winning at their *own* game, not the game devised by others, with the cards stacked in their favor.

## SHOCKPROOF ELEMENTS: LEADERSHIP, STRATEGY, ORGANIZATION, AND TALENT

Prioritizing the alignment between strategy, organization, talent, and leadership is the foundation for creating a Shockproof organization. Most organizations are multifaceted, and excelling in one, or even all of these areas fails to address the most critical issue—the issue of sustainability. Alignment among the elements contributes more to ongoing success than excellence in any one area, because the environment changes daily, and can quickly throw organizations out of balance.

In this book, we will describe and illustrate how leaders align strategy, organization, and talent to create lasting success (see Figure 1.1).

a. *Strategy:* What a company does to meet its objectives and create value.

b. *Organization:* The roles, activities, business processes, decision-making rights, and structure that must be in place to execute the strategy.

c. *Talent:* The people in the organization who do the work to execute strategy.

d. *Leadership:* The role leaders play to align and sustain the linkages between strategy, organization, and talent.

Every book ever written about business uses these terms, often with different meaning. When we use these terms to build Shockproof capability, here's how we define them:

**Figure 1.1   The Shockproof Model**

## *Strategy*

Business strategy is how companies intend to reach their stated objectives, creating value by differentiating themselves from competitors and focusing on the right markets and customers. There are seemingly endless approaches and battalions of business gurus available to companies to help them understand their customers, competition, and markets. Business books, some more readable than others, abound with diagnostic tools that can be used to assess market opportunity and identify relative strategic positioning, as a precursor to developing a plan for profitable growth. Most businesses take advantage of one form or another of the counsel available to them. On paper, many of these businesses have a decent strategic plan. These plans usually outline clear goals and objectives, desired market position, product mix, desired market share, and revenue and profit targets.

A strategic plan is important, but it's not enough. A thoughtful plan, elegant though it may be, must be absolutely workable. If your company doesn't have the capability and talent—or *chops*, as a jazz musician might say about another musician's ability to play an intricate chart—to execute a plan as written, then the investment in time, resources, and manpower will have been misspent because it is unlikely to work. Effective execution of a strategy requires painstaking realism and objectivity about the gap between where your business is today and what it will take to get it where you aspire to be tomorrow.

## *Organization*

Organization refers to how work is *designed* at the individual, team, and organizational levels—and the term is responsible for whole forests being cleared to supply enough paper to document thinking on the subject. With a quick Google search you will be inundated with contrasting and sometimes conflicting views on organization and how to get it right. Essentially, organization addresses the processes that are performed to execute the strategy, or as people often put it, "to get the job done." Organization design can include everything from core business processes that cut across multiple functions to how a particular job is designed in a customer service center, for example. Often grounded in engineering and production control disciplines, management thinkers have for some time been drawn to the idea of designing better work processes to improve the efficiency and quality of the products and services delivered by their companies. Methodologies like Six Sigma or Lean Manufacturing, for example, have been deployed to evolve work processes and reduce variance and waste while increasing efficiency and effectiveness. For most of us, we first think about structure when thinking about an organization. But structure is only one element of organization, and probably not the best place to begin to assess whether a company's organization design is fit for its purpose.

When Shockproof companies are fine-tuning or calibrating their organizations, they tackle areas of much greater impact than can be addressed by simply redrawing the boxes and lines or changing the players who occupy the boxes within a typical organization chart. Organization is about how people, functions, and processes interact to make products and deliver services. Clarifying the interactions that occur between people and functions in the white spaces *between* the boxes and lines often has a far greater impact on performance than redrawing the organization chart. How people work together, how decisions are made, how leaders lead, how customers are served, and how the processes can ensure effective execution are far more important than the organization chart. This white space between the boxes and lines is the "real estate" where the work of building effective organizations often takes place.

## *Talent*

Talent refers to either individuals who have unique and valued capabilities, or the collective skills and capabilities of a workforce. Over the years, management practices and theories have focused heavily on the people inside and outside organizations who are charged with carrying out the work necessary to successfully implement strategy. Important research has been conducted on the subject, including that by McKinsey & Company, published in 2001 as *The War for Talent*.[4] The authors advised companies "to recognize the strategic importance of human capital because of the enormous advantage that talent creates." That might seem to be a blinding flash of the obvious, but as with strategy and organization, there is an abundance of how-to resources available for organizations to learn how to better manage *talent*, who, after all, are *people!* Add to this a flood of talent management software applications that companies can use in an attempt to manage everything from employee sourcing and hiring to performance management and rewards. Many of these applications are promising; others are long on style but short on substance. Some applications make the strategic mistake of focusing on efficiency rather than effectiveness. They encourage leaders to focus on performance measures like "cost to hire" without assessing the effectiveness of new hires on the job. Ultimately, the way in which leaders manage talent has a tremendous influence on the extent to which they are Shockproof. Being Shockproof is about executing strategy effectively. And, since it is people who execute strategy, take author Jim Collins's advice and "make sure you have the right people on the bus."[5]

## *Leadership*

Shockproof leaders are transformational leaders. They are focused on how they and those they lead can grow and learn every day to improve strategy execution and results. They establish norms that encourage people to discuss successes and failures, and make it comfortable for them to ask for help from others on the team, not just the designated leader. These leaders encourage dialogue about what good leadership looks like, and they make sure that people are engaged in meaningful ways while adding value to the business. They value a feedback-rich culture, the benefits of change, and the growth that comes from understanding their own capabilities, motivations, and aspirations. They think systemically about the external competitive market and the internal capabilities needed to capitalize on opportunities and overcome challenges.

Shockproof leaders focus on breaking down the complexity in business today and helping colleagues and employees see the connections between what they do on a day-to-day basis and the company's path to success. These leaders ensure the ongoing alignment among strategy, organization, and talent. It's a significant responsibility, and not all leaders are

**Table 1.1   Shockproof Lens Definitions**

The *Systems Lens* enables people to see patterns and polarities in information that help to identify opportunities for improvement.

The *Value Lens* helps people continually attend to the true drivers of value and to revise their strategies and tactics as strategy evolves.

The *Change Lens* aids people to pay attention to the complex mechanics and dynamics of change situations.

The *Interpersonal Lens* assists people to inspire trust and respect through the skillful use of various communication methods.

The *Self-Awareness Lens* keeps people authentic, yet conscious of how their behaviors and actions are perceived by others.

naturally "tuned in" to see the connections or identify when they are out of sync. Shockproof leaders understand what creates value, and they know how to lead and manage change. They value and invest in building relationships. They appreciate the criticality of developing their own emotional intelligence and are comfortable with deep self-reflection. They exhibit five key capabilities, which we call the Shockproof Lenses. These will be briefly introduced here, in Table 1.1, and will subsequently be fully explored in later chapters.

## THE SHOCKPROOF MIND-SET AND CAPABILITIES

Three-dimensional glasses enhance the viewing experience for the moviegoer; similarly, business leaders must look through different lenses to create a Shockproof business or to effect real change. Leaders can train these lenses on the external competitive market and on every level of the organization and its people to assess necessary adjustments.

In addition to creative, nontraditional thinking, leaders need to develop deep business acumen to understand what actually *creates* and *sustains* value. Extending far beyond being able to understand the company's P&L, this requires an understanding of the activities and capabilities that must be executed to unlock and sustain value. Knowing what to focus on and what not to focus on, in equal measure is a strong sign of business acumen. And the top of the house can't be the only place where this acumen resides. It must be woven tightly throughout the depth and breadth of the organization to ensure an almost maniacal concentration on what drives the ultimate measure of value, whether it's total return to shareholders, EBITDA, or other concrete results. In some companies, the definition of value has evolved beyond financial results and value created for customers and employees to include consideration of the company's impact on the communities in which they operate. They must also understand how to successfully implement and manage change inside the company's four walls, as well as in the markets where it competes. Shockproof leaders also require a high degree of interpersonal competence and self-awareness. They need to be able to effectively communicate their ideas, get in touch with their own strengths and weaknesses, motivate their colleagues, become comfortable working collaboratively, and, ultimately, create a way for people to contribute to making something extraordinary happen.

When leaders consistently apply the Shockproof lenses in an effective manner, the company becomes hardwired to expect adjustments and calibrations, all aimed at creating value.

## CONNECTIONS AND CALIBRATIONS

Strategy, organization, talent, and leadership are the building blocks of a Shockproof company. Companies falter when they overinvest time and resources in one or two of these building blocks at the expense of the others. Leaders can avoid this faltering by intentionally engaging the right connections between the three building blocks. They also risk failing when they rest or stay "flat-footed," assuming that the connections require no further calibration or adjustment. The fact is that Shockproofing a business requires dynamically assessing and adjusting the connections to create alignment in response to challenges or opportunities. When this mindset becomes hardwired, people in the company won't even blink when a needed adjustment is suggested. In fact, they get used to change. They expect it and accept it. They accept change because leaders throughout the organization are on the same page about what the priorities are for customers and the business. They accept change because they would rather deal with dynamic changes and adjustments than unforeseen chaos. They accept change because they have experienced the incredible results that can be delivered by Shockproof companies, whether they are in turnaround situations, making course corrections, or, for the enviable few, sustaining profitable growth.

## THE SHOCKPROOF DIFFERENCE IN ACTION

The exciting glimpse into the future offered in the Prologue is not that far away from being realized today by leaders committed to calibrating the links between strategy, organization, and talent in their companies. These businesses are seeking and achieving better outcomes for shareholders, the planet, and for all people associated with the enterprise.

## Qualcomm Inc: Where Leaders Are Hardwired to Align Strategy with Organization and Talent

Qualcomm Incorporated is one of the best technology companies in the world. As of this writing, it sits shoulder to shoulder with Apple, Oracle, Accenture, and IBM as a top stock pick by Wall Street's most critical analysts. Though technological breakthroughs and rigorous intellectual property protection remain at the heart of the Qualcomm story, the *rest of the story* hinges on the thoughtful and intentional way talent has been managed and the organization has been designed over time to support Qualcomm's enduring sources of value creation. During Qualcomm's 25 years of climbing to the top of the NASDAQ, talent and organization strategies have also stretched and bent a bit, but not too far. Tamar Elkeles, PhD, in her role as the head of Learning at Qualcomm, comments that the "perseverance of a Qualcomm culture has been important to Qualcomm's success. The culture is one that is highly engineering-centric with a very heavy emphasis on promoting product and process innovation."[6] It is well documented that Qualcomm engineers are carefully selected not only for the match of their credentials and accomplishments with the current and emerging business needs, but for their ability to thrive in an environment that allows room for, and even demands, ambiguity, collaboration, and adaptation. "The business is organized around technologies to ensure depth of talent, at all times, within each technology group," Elkeles continues. Since Qualcomm grew so rapidly, most of its engineers were brought in from the outside, versus grown on the inside. After new engineers are signed on at Qualcomm, they are onboarded, deployed within their assigned technology group, mentored, and grown within their talent pool as preparation for new responsibilities. The goal has remained constant over time: "Develop the bench."

In its Finance Department, Qualcomm invested in a rotational program available to everyone in the talent pool, moving them through assignments in strategy, accounting, and tax. This has resulted in very well-rounded contributors who can be readily moved to a variety of roles as the business continues to expand. The Qualcomm way is to remove barriers to people performing at their potential. Learning is typically on demand, with few, if any, mandatory learning events. Experiences and spaces are created to help people collaborate and pursue innovation; and when practices or expectations creep up that interfere with the goals of the initiative, the culture is so strong the roadblocks are blasted through. People peak at different times in their careers, so talent pools allow for folks to either "bake" a bit longer or jump out of the frying pan and into a ready role. It is the role of HR to support the learning needs of those they serve. As needs pop up through affinity groups, climate surveys, and discussions with leadership, the HR organization explores the scope of the needs and then mobilizes the right cross-functional team to explore systemic solutions.

Because the company is designed to serve engineers and the technologies they support, silos tend to materialize, making collaboration challenging. However, rather than eradicate the silos for the sake of integration, HR works with the silos and creates other opportunities to move knowledge and networks outside of each silo. HR works to help their business partners see the needs of the business more systemically and less parochially, and to reward leaders for moving talent, versus hoarding resources. In some cases, they have been constrained in how they design the organization, based on SEC regulations and governance particular to their circumstances. Elkeles believes that Qualcomm's leaders are moving in the direction of being committed to the learning and development of others. This includes improved pay for performance that is linked to ensuring that the right talent can be made available as needs arise, and raising the awareness of leaders about the impact to the larger business of narrow decision making concerning talent. "Innovative learning approaches have helped keep the culture intact," Elkeles continues, "while stretching leaders to think beyond the boundaries of existing ways of getting results." These approaches include creative channels of distributed learning, among them 52 Weeks of Stories to help leaders learn from each other, award-winning online learning curricula, assessments, coaching, followership, and a variety of just-in-time learning solutions.

"We know that our ability to stay at the head of the pack is related to our skill at sourcing, attaining, engaging, and retaining top engineering talent, and all the functional resources that ensure that talent remain the best in the business," adds Dan Sullivan, PhD, EVP, Human Resources.[7] He also explains that "in Qualcomm's case, organization design and effectiveness links to the needs of our talent. Our talent ensures we drive home our strategic goals. It is a winning combination; our profitability and operating margins remain healthy and rising."

## WINNING ONCE VERSUS BEING SHOCKPROOF

We all know organizations that at some point in their life cycle win big and have a great success, fail outright, or make a comeback. Maybe the market conditions were favorable to their strategies, products, and services. In other instances, careful orchestration, planning, and alignment won the day.

While winning once is worth a tip of the hat, consistently adapting to survive and thrive is the real prize.

Driving an automobile that isn't in alignment over a prolonged period can result in a variety of short-term and longer-term negative effects: difficult steering, tire wear, poor fuel mileage. You might even have a blowout or, worse, an accident. A business's alignment between strategy, organization, and talent, once put in place, also requires constant vigilance and maintenance. It's a difficult leadership task for any company, large or small. And it requires a special mindset that isn't taught at B-school, and rarely, if ever, developed within most organizations. Having leaders align strategy, organization, and talent requires a seismic shift in traditional, discrete, mechanical "old-world" thinking about how businesses operate. It requires a more holistic and systemic understanding of the interplay between strategy, organization, and talent. It is much more than thinking outside the box. There is no box.

Ultimately, *Shockproof* is about the journey that leaders in organizations take to shape themselves and their organizations. It isn't an easy or simple path, but it is well worth taking. Organizations that take this path continually evolve to overcome challenges and capitalize on opportunities. The customer-facing organization becomes more agile and responsive in the best sort of way—meeting customer needs and the needs of the organization at the same time. R&D becomes immediately relevant, and picks up pace because of a strong link to what customers actually want, versus what engineers would like to create. Leaders' lives are both easier and more challenging: Their organizations are increasingly self-led and accountability-driven; but at the same time, people challenge their leaders. The leader is joined on his or her journey by everyone in the organization, sharing ownership and holding the leader's feet to the fire to live up to standards they themselves set.

Many entities, public, private, or not-for-profit, routinely rely on the talent of experts to achieve their objectives. It's only well-intended human nature that leads people to develop expertise so they can contribute to their workplaces and communities. As a result, we often build our identities around what we know and do best, and design organizations and work processes accordingly. Or, we create corporate strategy teams and hire consultants to craft *the* optimal strategy. We focus on process improvements or change strategies to reduce errors and speed up time-to-market. We build world-class corporate universities and hire the best faculty to teach our employees. Then we "spin" the business media, feeding them the easy-to-tell type of story they love, about the corporate silver bullet we used to solve a thorny problem, all in the hope that the subsequent publicity will garner us "great place to work" or "most admired" status.

The problem with media-driven image making is that it is, at best, an incomplete or one-dimensional perspective, if not self-serving. By focusing on the individual elements of strategy, organization, and talent, rather than on how they are interconnected, and relying on experts in each discipline or element, organizations risk missing the opportunity for long-term success. Like the blind man and the elephant, they fail to see the whole picture. Thus, as the environment changes, most companies fail to change *holistically*. People in Shockproof companies, however, realize that new challenges require them to constantly consider what they need to do, how they should do it, and who should do it. Rather than fighting to survive the forces of change, they welcome change as the lifeblood of their organizations. These companies thrive on uncertainty, while others wither; they overcome when others stumble; and they are held up by their peers as examples of resilience and sustainability.

## THE JOURNEY BEGINS

In *Shockproof: How to Hardwire Your Business for Lasting Success*, we outline an integrated approach to help leaders make the right connections between strategy, organization, and talent. We equip leaders with a new way of thinking about and seeing their businesses in a more integrated and holistic way, through a set of five unique *lenses*.

We provide practical insights, examples, and anecdotes describing how leaders connect the elements and adjust or calibrate the connections. Our hope is that you will come away with a belief we share: That resilient trumps disposable, and that incubating and propagating the Shockproof mindset to build sustainable, profitable organizations is the new responsibility of leaders.

So read on.

Keep the big blue catfish at bay. Let him circle and then watch him give up and dart away.

# CHAPTER 2

## *Headlines or Tombstones?*

That some achieve great success is proof to
all that others can achieve it as well.
—Abraham Lincoln

U.S. Postal Service Reports $1.6 Billion
Quarter Loss
—BLOOMBERG

FedEx Corp. Increases Earnings Outlook
—WALL STREET JOURNAL

Can Crocs Be More Than a One-Hit
Wonder?
—TIME

Nike Sees Sales Up 40 Percent by 2015
—REUTERS

BearingPoint Seeks Bankruptcy Protection
—WASHINGTON POST

Carlyle's Booz Allen Hamilton Seeks $300
Million IPO
—BLOOMBERG BUSINESSWEEK

The business press never blinks. Good news. Bad news. No news. It's all fair game for the 24-hour news cycle, which has a ravenous appetite, and thousands of stories are produced every day for its consumption. Conditioned to this, business leaders often worry about "staying off the front page," unless of course their news is positive, in which case they want the world to know. And most would agree with Edward R. Murrow who famously said, "We cannot make good news out of bad practice,"[1] so there's added pressure to perform. As observers and news consumers, we're in the catbird seat, able to watch and learn from the experiences of others.

So what's to be learned from the successes and failures of the businesses and leaders that have gone before us? What distinguishes the winners from the losers? The one-hit wonders from the classics? For every Eric Clapton there are thousands of Tommy Tutones, and the difference is less in what they do and more in how they do it. Great businesses, like great musicians, are able to remain relevant by consistently evolving while at the same time continuing to play to their strengths and deliver something that their audiences love and expect. They have to be bold, yet not lose sight of the fundamentals, and they must maintain excellence in their craft while attending to how the pieces fit together around them.

## AFTER A WHILE, CROCODILE . . .

If you're not familiar with the product Crocs, you either don't have children or are one of those rare people who look straight ahead (not down) when you walk. Crocs are

25

the colorful shoes named after crocodiles, for their amphib-
ian qualities: Good on land. Completely waterproof.
Lightweight, comfortable, odor resistant, relatively inexpen-
sive. Children love them. So do adults—from your next-door
neighbor to George Clooney, Rosie O'Donnell, and former
President George W. Bush.

Founded in 1999, Crocs, Inc., revenues went from
$24,000 in 2002 to $847 million in 2007. The February 2006
IPO raised $208 million, which is the single biggest IPO of
a shoe manufacturer in history. In 2007, Crocs reported a
profit of $168 million.

Then the shock hit. Consumer demand for the shoes
fell off; the recession kicked in hard, and sales fell. The share
price dropped from a high point of $74.00 in November 2007
to a low of $1.04 a year later, and the company recorded a
loss of $185 million for 2008. While 2008 was a bad year for
most companies, it was an especially bad year for Crocs. With
one core product and an adoring fan base, Crocs behaved
like a young rock star with its first hit song, spending more
money than it should have and not evolving to keep its fans
engaged.

This has not been lost on Crocs. The company has
brought on new leadership and is expanding its product
line. It has also closed factories, reduced inventory, and cut
jobs substantially. As of May 2010 the stock was trading
at over $11.00.[2]

## IS IT THE SHOES?

Far from a one-hit wonder, Nike has made the transition
from specialty running shoe distributor, which outfitted
track teams and competitive runners, to full-blown athletics

juggernaut, designing and selling footwear, apparel, and accessories to athletes worldwide. Instead of remaining a niche brand, Nike has co-branded products with Apple, licensed the song "Revolution" from the Beatles (definitely *not* a one-hit wonder), and ingrained its brand in popular culture through its "Just Do It" tagline.

Nike is worn by athletes in almost every sport around the world, from weekend warriors to elite amateurs and top-tier professionals. Golfers including Lucas Glover, K.J. Choi, and, of course, Tiger Woods have won major tournaments playing with Nike golf clubs and balls (a product category Nike entered, along with footwear and apparel, in the 1990s). Serena Williams, Rafael Nadal, Maria Sharapova, and Roger Federer wear Nike's tennis togs. Hundreds of college sports teams are outfitted in Nike wear, from head to toe. The company's cleats provide traction to the Green Gators U8 girls' soccer team in McLean, Virginia, as well as to top players on the, Spanish, Dutch, Brazilian, United States, English, and Korean 2010 World Cup national teams.

Nike's broad customer base is loyal and active, often purchasing products for different age groups and sports and seasons, thereby growing revenue potential and spreading the risk of market cycles (such as golf's boom and bust between the 1990s and 2010). Few companies can boast Nike's global appeal and caché, and its vision drives its success.

During a May 2010 investor meeting, the company announced that it would grow revenue by more than 40 percent, to $27 billion, by 2015, and do so profitably. "We've never been more inspired, innovative, and aligned to achieve our goals," said Nike, Inc., President and CEO Mark Parker. "We have powerful competitive advantages in our portfolio— innovative and compelling products, brands that are distinct and relevant to their consumers, and the world's greatest athletes and teams. Our focus is to build, fuel, and accelerate the power of our portfolio."[3]

Meanwhile, Crocs has been traveling the bumpy road back, returning to profitability in Q1 of 2010. In a press release announcing these results, John McCarvel, Crocs' new President and Chief Executive Officer said that, "Revenues improved across all channels and across each region this quarter, driven by strong customer reception to our products. . . . Margins also improved as we benefitted from our cost-savings initiatives undertaken in 2009. Our strategy to return to profitable growth in 2010 has not changed, and this positive start to the year positions us well to execute against that plan."[4] The company's intent seems clear, but it will be its execution over time that will make the difference.

## NEITHER SNOW NOR RAIN NOR HEAT NOR GLOOM OF NIGHT . . .

The United States Postal Service (USPS) was at one time, a U.S. Cabinet-level organization, and the Postmaster General was in the presidential line of succession. An enormous organization, the USPS employs more than 600,000 people and has well over 200,000 vehicles and 36,500 retail facilities. Founded by Benjamin Franklin more than 235 years ago, the USPS is an organization that has stood the test of time. But is it Shockproof? Not likely.

According to a 2010 IBM Global Business Services study conducted by Norma Nieto, Keith Strange, and William Takis ("Strategic Responses to Recession: A Comparison of the U.S. Postal Service to Other Leading Companies"), the USPS "experienced significant declines in the demand for its products and services, resulting in . . . revenue losses of over 9 percent in 2009 [and] . . . a corresponding decline in net income . . . [of] $3.8 billion lost. . . . However, while many other companies suffered similar revenue declines during this recession, few exhibited this proportional level of net losses." The IBM study indicates that "the lingering negative net income exhibited by the Postal Service is atypical—most other companies rebounded with positive net incomes within one or two quarters after a relatively short period of losses."[5]

True, the U.S. economy was in recession at this time, so you would expect most businesses to suffer poor results. This macroeconomic shift was not lost on the IBM consultants, who compared the USPS to the Fortune 500, pointing out that "while average net incomes for the Fortune 500 recovered quickly, net income for the Postal Service has continued to stagnate." And it's not that the USPS was asleep at the wheel. According to IBM, the USPS "took unprecedented steps to reduce both labor and capital expenses throughout 2008 and 2009 . . . [and while] those steps were similar to those taken by many of the leading companies in their efforts to rapidly restore net incomes . . . they were not sufficient to restore and sustain positive net income levels" for the USPS. Refining their comparison of the USPS's performance "to firms in the Fortune 500 with similar cost structures in the mail, package, and freight industry [FedEx, UPS, Deutsche Post, and TNT]," IBM found "results for these companies to be "strikingly similar to those of other sectors/industries. Despite severe initial and lingering revenue erosion, net income for these USPS competitors bounced back quickly."

The IBM study concludes is that while the USPS has taken "unprecedented strides in the area of cost control, [it] has failed in restoring its net income position because

it does not have the regulatory/legislative flexibility necessary to manage its business through economic shocks."
According to IBM, the USPS is hampered by excessive
political and regulatory oversight that restricts the organization's ability to shed costs quickly in the face of economic
shocks—particularly when compared to its competitors
such as FedEx, UPS, and others. In closing, the researchers state that "the empirical results are clear. Whether the
comparison is between the [USPS] and the Fortune 500 as
a whole, or similar subsectors, other companies have been
better able to respond to the economic shocks imposed by
the most recent recession."

## FEDEX DELIVERS

As IBM observed, commercial carriers do not face the same
constraints as the USPS and, as a result, are in a better position
to resist shocks. FedEx Chief Executive Officer Fred Smith
begins his 2009 letter to shareholders with the following: "In
times like these, it's easy for companies to let the economy
manage them. It's easy to get swept up in putting out the next
fire. It's easy to think short term. But FedEx has always been
focused on the future, and we believe tough times only punc-
tuate the need to think long term. Accordingly, we continue
to look at what the world of commerce needs for the long
haul, even when the economy is in a recession."[6]

The package delivery industry is considered by many
experts to be a bellwether of the general economy because
package shipments are driven by activity between businesses
and their customers. As a leader in package delivery, FedEx's
results track accordingly. So when the recession hit hard in
2008, FedEx felt the shock. As noted previously, this shock
affected leading shippers similarly, and their response was—
not surprisingly—to cut costs in an effort to remain afloat.

A logistics-driven business founded by an ex-Marine, FedEx was targeted and swift in its response, and has been frequently cited as a great example of American ingenuity and entrepreneurship. Importantly, FedEx went beyond just reducing costs; it took the opportunity to optimize its routes and equipment, consolidate facilities, and refocus aircraft purchases to better match demand. As CEO Smith said in the 2009 annual report, the company realigned its "organization and resources to concentrate on those things that matter most." Smith's approach was effective and grounded in his expectation of continuous change because, as he told the Academy of Achievement, he has rarely "seen any business or major undertaking . . . [go] in a straight line."

According to FedEx's 2009 annual report, the company also tightened control over discretionary expenses such as travel, entertainment, and professional fees; cut pay for U.S. salaried personnel; suspended its 401(k) match; eliminated bonus payouts; and froze hiring. Tough medicine, and surprisingly well understood by FedEx's workforce, who helped keep the company on *Fortune's* 100 Best Companies to Work For, 12 times in 13 years.

While these measures required sacrifice, FedEx's employees understood and supported them because they are aligned with the company's strategy, and they believe in its People, Service, Profit (PSP) mantra. As described by Smith to the Academy of Achievement, PSP is instrumental in the company's success. PSP, he said, "insists that our people be treated fairly" and that "if we give good service and come up with a reasonable profit, we make that a good deal for our employees. If you're going to run a high service organization, you have to get the commitment of the people working for that organization right at the start." And according to Smith, it was because of the extraordinary efforts of FedEx's employees that the company "weathered the stormy economy better than most."[7]

In closing his 2009 letter to shareholders, Smith says that, "Despite the strong economic headwinds, we are building on our strengths to produce outstanding results when the recovery occurs. We've built shock absorbers into our networks—that is, the ability to flex up or down as economic conditions and volumes shift. It gives us the resiliency to power through hard times like the present. We are rich in committed people. Our team members are the best in the industry, always ready to serve our customers and communities. In fact, we have continued to improve service levels during this tough economy. Our leadership team is more focused and collaborative than at any time in our history."

And while—as the small print in every investment prospectus notes—forward-looking statements are subject to certain risks and uncertainties, it appears that FedEx is proving its ability to respond to shocks. On March 18, 2010, the company reported third-quarter earnings of $0.76 per diluted share, compared to $0.31 the year before. Revenue was up 7 percent, operating income up 129 percent, net income up 146 percent; and operating margin more than doubled, leading the company to raise its earnings forecast for the fiscal year ending in May of 2010. A month later, FedEx's Board of Directors increased the quarterly dividend, while other companies were cutting back or eliminating their dividends, signaling its optimism to investors, employees, and customers.

## CONSULTANT, HEAL THYSELF

Spun off from international accounting giant KPMG in a $2 billion 2001 IPO, BearingPoint (then KPMG Consulting) grew rapidly, investing significantly and hiring top talent.

As the post-Sarbanes-Oxley era progressed, BearingPoint did, too, acquiring firms throughout the world, as well as enormous debt along the way. A string of strategic blunders drained cash and distracted leadership, and very little of its IPO cash was put back into the business. Staff-level turnover soared, and talk around its McLean, Virginia, headquarters turned from *if* the firm would fail to *when* it would fail.

Efforts were made to sell parts of the firm to keep it afloat; but as a publicly traded company, its stock took a beating. A series of financial restatements and 10 CFOs in nine years were ultimately the firm's undoing. The company filed for Chapter 11 bankruptcy on February 18, 2009, and in May of that year sold its government consulting business to Deloitte for $350 million. The firm survives in name only as BearingPoint Europe Holdings B.V.[8]

What went wrong? While it would appear that BearingPoint's rapid succession of leaders was focused on growing the firm, they failed to effectively align strategy, organization, and talent, and were ultimately "shocked" right out of business.

On the other hand, Accenture and Booz Allen Hamilton are two dramatically different stories. Similar to BearingPoint, Accenture started out as the former consulting division of a public accounting firm (Arthur Andersen), and has grown to more than 190,000 people. Accenture leverages its Business Integration Methodology to coordinate people, process, technology, and strategy to deliver consulting services to its clients around the world. Breck Marshall, an Accenture Management Consulting senior executive, says this approach "goes back to the firm's accounting roots, where in order to deliver complex accounting services well, our approach was to 'lock down' methods and procedures necessary to execute the work. So, when we entered the systems business, we realized we had so many people working that we needed a way to coordinate them. So we emphasized process, and this has stuck with us."[9]

This approach serves Accenture well in managing projects that are staggering in their scale. U.S. Federal Sales Executive Ed Meehan adds, "An Accenture system goes live every four hours and, today, half of the world's mail goes through Accenture supported systems, and one third of the world's mobile phone bills are created on a system that Accenture developed."[10]

Many businesses of this size collapse under their own weight. Unable to evolve to keep up with their customers, they fall prey to what Clayton Christensen terms "disruptive innovation." In his best-selling book, *The Innovator's Dilemma*, Christensen describes how established firms in industries ranging from disk drives to steel manufacturing and retail have been displaced by agile upstarts that are minimally invested in the status quo, because established firms fall prey to "disruptive innovation," an inability to keep up with their customers.[11] Accenture is keenly aware of this potential pitfall, and as Breck Marshall puts it, "Our mantra has been to reevaluate and reinvent ourselves before the competition catches up. Sometimes it can be painful—taking a very successful business and repositioning it instead for long-term success."

Betty Thompson, Booz Allen Hamilton's Senior Vice President of People Services, also gets it. "It's difficult to think about change when things are going well. Success can be the biggest obstacle companies have to wrestle with. I think the reason Booz Allen has been so successful is because the consultant in all of us likes to examine things, to pull things apart, make changes so that we can stay ahead of the curve."

This thinking was evident in the firm's 2008 decision to separate its commercial and government consulting divisions. The firm grew for more than 90 years until July 31, 2008, when it sold a majority stake in the U.S. government consulting business to the Carlyle Group for $2.54 billion. According to Thompson, "Both sides of the business had continued to grow—the government side in particular was very successful, and we realized that if we kept going down this path we wouldn't be as successful. Up until then we had common people management programs and practices, and many of them were driven by the commercial business because two thirds of the officers were in the commercial business, even though the largest part of our business was in government." For years the firm had worked hard to "leverage the best of both . . . but ultimately the differences were too great," continues Thompson. "We had different career models, different motivations . . . the beauty of it was that this was recognized before it became a negative."

Upon separation of the businesses, the People Services team set about establishing the foundations for managing talent in the new Booz Allen Hamilton. Says Thompson, "I believe that what distinguishes great companies is that they see big changes as opportunities and do not panic. We saw the opportunity to take things further by aligning our people programs appropriately to our business. We identified our key business drivers and realized that one of our priorities was to develop more leaders faster, to support our plans for double-digit growth."

Looking back, says Thompson, "We changed a lot of things. It was really about taking a step back and figuring out what the people strategy was that would optimize this business, while being mindful not to throw the baby out with the bathwater. People love working here and we didn't want that to change."

One of the things that has remained constant at Booz Allen is its consulting roots. "Maintaining our consulting legacy is very important; so is keeping the focus on people development, caring about their careers and giving them the opportunity to grow as the business grows," explains Thompson. "We are different, and we like the fact that we are different; and that's what makes us successful, even when others are retreating. The firm has grown from 16,000 employees to 22,000 in the two years I have been here, and our strategy is to continue to grow."

Similarly, Accenture's Meehan says that what he thinks "is remarkable is how [Accenture's] culture stays so strong, while bringing 30,000 to 50,000 new people a year in to the business." Hired fresh from undergraduate school at Santa Clara University in Santa Clara, California, he recalls that when he came on board "90 percent of the people who joined the firm were campus hires, and now it's almost the reverse." He goes on to say that Accenture has evolved for the better. "It's a very different place, but retains that cultural bond. We hire people who have an affinity for the work we do, but they come from different places, and once they're on the team we're *that much better immediately*. . . . [W]e're not looking for people who are just like us; we're looking for people with different ways of thinking that are conducive to serving clients and tapping the collective knowledge of the firm in a different way."

## COULD THIS BE YOU?

See if you can guess the company who's 2009 Letter to Shareholders is excerpted below.

Dear Fellow Shareholders:
In my letter to you a year ago, I stated that in light of the severe macroeconomic conditions

confronting the business, our goal for 2009 was to preserve the Company's financial core while positioning us to take full advantage of opportunities as these conditions moderated. Our objective was to emerge a stronger Company—not just a survivor.

To accomplish this objective, we focused the organization on three areas of our business: (1) preserving the strength of the balance sheet by improving our cash flow profile and driving down debt; (2) putting the needs of customers first by ensuring them that we would remain a stable and secure supply partner; and (3) reminding each employee that [our] PEOPLE matter, and that they can make a difference through continuous cost reduction, improved business processes, and active collaboration.

I am proud to report to you today that we not only achieved our goals—we exceeded them. 2009 was an excellent year for [our company], with both strong financial results and notable operational success. Our performance was a testament to the soundness of our strategy, the strength and resilience of our specialized business model, and the commitment of [our] PEOPLE around the world. For [our company], the story of 2009 is one of precise strategic execution, which drove solid results, thereby positioning our business to enter 2010 with renewed momentum. Not many companies that I know of can make that claim. And I think that's a strong statement to our shareholders. . . .

In many ways, the results speak for themselves . . . while others were internally focused and distracted, [our company] had the management capacity, financial flexibility, and courage to seek out opportunities to further advance our long-term strategy. . . . Creating indelible linkage between operating strategy and business results—that is the reason [our company] is a stronger Company today than when I last wrote to you one year ago.

## Long-Term View

[We] know that uncertain times offer unique opportunity for organizations focused upon a clear plan. 2009 was not the toughest year we've ever faced, and it won't be the last tough year to come. The hallmark of a sustainable organization is found in its ability to survive and grow stronger through generational challenges. 2009 was yet another step in our journey. In summary, while external influences caused us to modify our operating strategy early in 2009, the results we generated simply could not have happened without the solid performance and deep commitment of [our company's] PEOPLE everywhere. Most rewarding to me is that our success in large part resulted from improved business processes and principles of continuous improvement that are now embedded in the organization. By implementing the operating strategy to drive results, we not only delivered strong financial performance in 2009, but also emerged with clear momentum for our future. . . .[12]

These are truly impressive achievements in the face of impossible odds and in the depths of a global recession: This company beat the odds, and beat them handily.

Because we have removed references to the company's name from this letter, you might assume that it is a large and famous business you're familiar with, led by a rock star CEO whose achievements have been splashed across the covers of *Fortune, BusinessWeek*, and *Forbes*. Or perhaps it's an Internet hotrod in its infancy and led by a 20-something wunderkind. At the very least, it must be an emerging player in a new industry, like renewable energy. How else could it deliver such results?

Well, you'd be surprised. Our hero is P.H. Glatfelter Company, a $1.4 billion producer of specialty papers and engineered products, headquartered in York, Pennsylvania. With manufacturing facilities in the United States, Canada, Europe, and the Philippines, Glatfelter employs more than 4,200 people worldwide. The company was started by Philip H. Glatfelter in 1864, and since 2000 has been led by Chairman and CEO George H. Glatfelter II, the founder's great-great grandson.

That's right: a paper company. With substantial U.S.-based manufacturing facilities, led by a descendent of the founder. Here's Glatfelter's headline:

Glatfelter Has the Highest Gross Margin in the
Paper Products Industry
—INVESTORS.COM (INVESTOR'S BUSINESS DAILY)

From modest beginnings nearly 150 years ago as a paper pulp business, Glatfelter has established itself as a leader in innovation, with more than 50 percent of its revenue coming from products introduced within the past five years. And, while not a household name, the company counts among its clients Procter & Gamble and Johnson & Johnson. Its plants produce over 60 percent of the world's tea bags, and Glatfelter is a leader in such specialty paper markets as book paper, carbonless paper, playing card stock, and metalized papers such as those found on premium beer labels. As Bill Yanavitch, Glatfelter's Vice President of Human Resources & Administration put it, "We touch people every day, but you'll never hear our name."

## GLATFELTER GOES BEYOND PAPER

In business for a century and a half, it's no surprise that Glatfelter has hit a few bumps in the road. Whereas the company survived the Great Depression, 1972's Hurricane Agnes dealt a severe blow to Glatfelter's operations and financial conditions. The company rebuilt and then made a series of acquisitions, entering the recycled printing paper business in 1979 and the tobacco paper business in 1987. These moves paid off in the short run, until the market for tobacco paper began to turn, first when Philip Morris made the decision to single-source its tobacco paper from Kimberly-Clark Corporation, and then throughout the decade as cigarette consumption dropped and tobacco liability lawsuits led cigarette companies to put more pressure on their suppliers. By the late 1990s, while the U.S. economy was robust, Glatfelter was suffering. The company tried to sell its tobacco paper business, but the offers were so low it instead decided to write down its value. This was followed by painful layoffs, in an effort to return the company to financial stability.[13]

So how did Glatfelter, a company founded near Gettysburg, Pennsylvania, shortly after the famous Civil War battle, stay alive while under attack from outside forces? Glatfelter's Bill Yanavitch is keenly aware of this risk. "We could have died," he said, "like any one of the hundred or so U.S. paper companies that have disappeared during the recent past."[14]

Much of the credit for seeing the light of another business day goes to Chairman and CEO, George H. Glatfelter II. Descended from the company's founder, Glatfelter became Chairman in 2000 after serving as its President and CEO since 1998, and holding positions in Human Resources, Maintenance and Engineering, Operations, Planning, and Sales and Marketing. He succeeded Thomas Norris, a Glatfelter veteran who had taken the reigns upon the retirement of George's grandfather, in 1980. George Glatfelter II knew the business inside out and realized that though the company had a long and rich history, it also faced an uncertain future. Many of its products were advanced in their life cycles, and Glatfelter was increasingly counting on mature and eroding products such as tobacco filters to meet its financial objectives. Competing in increasingly commoditized markets, Glatfelter felt pressure on its profitability, and its eponymous CEO determined that it was time to begin doing things differently.

Bill Yanavitch joined the company in 2000, as the pace of change was quickening. "Off profile," for a senior executive at the time, Yanavitch didn't come from the paper industry, and he was facing challenging times as Glatfelter's new Human Resources leader. Margins had eroded to the point where the company went several years without paying bonuses, and employees weren't seeing fully the connection. Yanavitch realized that connecting the dots between Glatfelter's people and the changing world around them would be critical in supporting the changes that were to come. Working closely with CEO Glatfelter and the senior executive team, he and other leaders at the company began making it a priority to share with employees more information about the company and its industry. Glatfelter and his team began "letting employees know what challenges we faced requiring fundamental changes to the way we operated the Company," said Yanavitch. "Employees didn't trust this at first. Senior management had to learn to tell the story in a way that people could understand." In the early days, "the leadership team made the rounds . . . and won people over by honoring their core values," added Yanavitch. Demonstrating his commitment to the future and to his workforce, George Glatfelter, for example, declined his annual bonus and asked the board of directors to redistribute these funds toward a high-performance award for employees.

During these difficult times, Glatfelter made a series of bold moves designed to position the company for the future. He sold off timberlands that the company had owned for years to raise money to pay down debt and prepare for future growth. The businesses he bought were identified because they increased the company's profit potential while leveraging its operational strengths. In 2006, Glatfelter made the first of a series of transformational acquisitions, purchasing a carbon-less paper business in Chillicothe, Ohio. Next, the company divested an underperforming recycled printing paper facility, bought a bankrupt U.K.-based composite fibers business and invested in equipment to improve its performance.

Like many long-standing U.S. manufacturers, Glatfelter's history was steeped in research and operations. "We were good at what we did—making paper—and didn't think much about developing new products," said Yanavitch. "George [Glatfelter II] believed that the company should 'go beyond paper,' and in order to make that vision a reality we needed to get closer to our customers, and partner with them to develop new products. Going beyond paper was how George Glatfelter communicated our move from commodities to higher-margin specialty products."

But the company couldn't do this on its own. Bill Yanavitch recounts that, "We made a choice to get closer to our customers and ask them to tell us what they needed. We also began bringing new talent on board, who brought with them experience in innovation. For example, a new senior executive who had a strong track record in new product development introduced new processes to the company and helped us streamline the key processes. Under his leadership, we built a stronger product pipeline around the globe, and today the company's new products drive our profits. Customers seek us out because we are willing to invest in niche markets and react quickly to meet their specialized needs. And, if we can't solve a customer's problem, we partner with them to find someone who can."

As the company evolved, Glatfelter and Yanavitch realized the need to make changes at the leadership level, as well. According to Yanavitch, "George had the courage to make big changes and let some people go who had helped teach him the paper business and supported his career." At the same time, Yanavitch stepped up hiring, bringing into Glatfelter people with new perspectives about customer and supplier intimacy, labor relations, and workforce engagement. The strategy has been successful, and financial analysts who track Glatfelter's stock recognize the value of the management team. As Yanavitch says, "We have learned the discipline to execute well," and make it a priority to align the company's strategic and operating goals and share financial and other key performance information with all employees, continuously. Employees are engaged, and it shows in their results. And as George Glatfelter notes on the company's web site, "Going beyond paper means that our people, already committed to excellence, aspire to exceed expectations."

## READ YOUR NEXT HEADLINE, USING SHOCKPROOF LENSES

Businesses, as we know, are not living, breathing beings. Although we ascribe to them human characteristics like, *innovative, environmentally conscious, resilient, creative*, or even *evil*, businesses themselves simply aren't human. However, the results they produce are generated by people and led by people. It is these people—leaders—who can have the greatest and most visible impact on their businesses' ability to achieve lasting success. Like George Glatfelter, Nike's Phil Knight, and FedEx's Fred Smith, the visions, values, and personal attributes of their leaders are essential in helping businesses respond to shocks.

Fred Smith shares a common view, among what we refer to as Shockproof leaders, that nothing is static, and that conditions, people, and learning change on a daily basis. As Smith writes in FedEx's 2009 annual report, "Putting our team members' interests first—and giving them the power to see and respond to what their customers need—was arguably the best business decision we ever made."

In a Shockproof business, as evidenced by the examples of Nike and FedEx, leaders attend to the connections among strategy, organization, and talent. Because they take a systems perspective, understand sources of true value creation, are committed to real change mastery, appreciate the criticality of developing their own emotional intelligence, and are naturally self-reflective, these leaders are better than most at helping Shockproof the businesses they lead. To achieve these results, they rely on, and look through, what we refer to as the five Shockproof Lenses (see Figure 2.1).

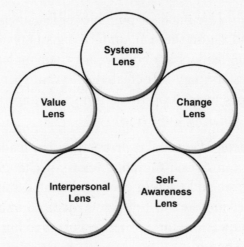

**Figure 2.1  Shockproof Lenses**

We call them *lenses* because they inform how Shockproof leaders view themselves and the world around them. They help leaders *see more and see differently*. Like an eagle that can see for miles, or an owl with powerful night vision, Shockproof Leaders can use their heightened senses to help their businesses succeed over the long term. Unlike these birds of prey, which cannot teach other birds how to see in this way, these leaders *can* share their lenses with others, effectively extending their field of vision to entire communities of people. By seeing more and seeing differently, and helping others to do the same, these leaders use the lenses that are described below to align strategy, organization, and talent.

*The Systems Lens* provides leaders with a wide-angle, panoramic perspective that helps them to see the dynamic relationships and connections that exist among business units, functions, processes, technology, and people inside the organization, as well as with external stakeholders (i.e., suppliers, customers, communities and regulators).

*The Value Lens* makes it possible for leaders to see, prioritize, and act on the real, underlying and primary sources of value; leaders are able to use their understanding of business strategy to defeat the "tyranny of the urgent" and focus instead on those things that are most important to creating long-term value.

*The Change Lens* makes it possible for leaders to zoom in and out to see the complexity of change situations; the degree and pace of change that an organization can tolerate; and the most effective methods to align people, communications, and other resources to implement successful change.

*The Interpersonal Lens* makes it possible for leaders to see how to best understand, empathize, and connect with people to forge relationships that combine trust, mutual respect, and learning.

*The Self-Awareness Lens* makes it possible for leaders to look in the mirror to gain insight into self, including strengths and weaknesses, personality, style preferences, interests, and values.

The Shockproof Lenses will be more fully described and illustrated throughout this book. For now, keep in mind that each lens is powerful on its own; but when coupled with one or more of the other lenses, the positive effect expands exponentially.

## THE FUTURE IS NOW: LET'S GET STARTED

The next time you read the paper or watch the news, ask yourself who you would rather be working for: Crocs or Nike? The U.S. Postal Service or FedEx? BearingPoint or Booz Allen Hamilton or Accenture? Glatfelter, or any number of famous but declining companies that are losing ground to more focused and agile competitors, and risk going out of business with every passing day?

The U.S. Postal Service was founded around the time of the American revolution—yet today its future is uncertain. It may be hamstrung by statutory, regulatory, and appropriations restrictions, but it is precisely its inability to make bolder moves to better align strategy, talent, and organization with today's economic realities that threaten its future.

Crocs and BearingPoint had their day in the sun, but weren't able to sustain their success. The distractions of early success and flawed initial responses to financial missteps were (in the case of BearingPoint) insurmountable. Barriers may have existed between the C-suite and the front lines, and it is possible that this disconnect kept employees and leaders from realizing their common interests. The best intentions of a misaligned workforce proved insufficient to sustain these companies' early successes. And by trying to salvage their businesses tactically, introducing new strategies, shifting organization design, or making changes to talent, leaders missed the opportunity to maintain the connection between these three drivers of business success. These organizations have hit some big bumps in the road and have been jarred by the shock. In some cases, they didn't anticipate change and waited too long to respond. In others, leaders were unable to distinguish the important from the trivial and wasted valuable resources pursuing initiatives that were not vital to their success.

Shockproofing is a new mind-set built upon the tried and true, with a good dose of discipline and focus mixed in. Many organizations and their leaders may have experienced the power of Shockproofing without ever using this term. We encourage these organizations and their leaders to own their success, to build on their experience, and to continue focusing on the alignment between strategy, organization, and talent. For those to whom these ideas are new, we welcome you with enthusiasm, and encourage you to look for and build upon that which is familiar. Hardwiring your business for lasting success is easier than it may seem, but more difficult than you might hope. It requires an awareness of what works and, more importantly, a willingness to apply proven approaches in new ways.

In the pages that follow, we will share stories about organizations and leaders that have already applied the principles of Shockproofing. From high-fashion brands to not-for-profit organizations, from ad agency executives to an Air Force One officer and the guys who bring you Corona beer, these leaders will show you how they have aligned strategy, organization, and talent to generate enviable results. We invite you to read this book through their lenses.

# CHAPTER 3

# *Make Sure the Strategy Is "Not Wrong"*

No battle plan survives contact with the enemy.
—Helmuth von Moltke

On May 24, 2010, IBM announced that it had agreed to acquire Sterling Commerce, a business-to-business (B2B) software applications provider from AT&T, for $1.4 billion.[1] At IBM's 2010 investor meeting, CEO Samuel Palmisano announced a reboot of the company's strategy and its intent to gain greater share in software applications.[2] This is not an insignificant shift, as IBM is planning for software to represent half of the company's pretax profits by 2015. It's perhaps as big a reboot as the change implemented by Lou Gerstner, IBM's CEO from 1993 to 2002, who led the shift in the company's focus from hardware into services.

Bob Irwin, the CEO of Sterling Commerce since 2007, takes a very straightforward approach to strategy in saying that, "The most important aspect of strategy is to make sure it's 'not wrong.'"[3] Underlying this comment is a belief that companies overinvest in the analytical process of trying to get their strategies perfect and don't put enough effort into implementation. Irwin believes, "You should get the strategy to a place where you're confident that it's *not wrong*, and then get everybody focused on execution." That's not to say that Irwin lacks an appreciation for data analysis and rigorous rounds of scenario planning, but he knows when to draw a line under the analytical process, declare it complete, and move on.

On the face of it, the conventional wisdom on business strategy is pretty straightforward. Hundreds of business books are sold every year that describe successful companies and their strategies, packaging their insights into digestible bites.

Countless biographies and autobiographies chart the journeys of superstar leaders who saved the day with a brilliant strategy; and case studies on strategy and competitive positioning frame highly rational arguments about what it takes to win. And for every winning business, there's a loser. Books, blogs, and the popular press are ready, willing, and able to diagnose and dissect how and where the "wheels came off" companies that were once great but ultimately ground to a standstill.

The bottom line is that the science behind strategy and how to formulate it—what is commonly referred to as *Strategy IQ*—is widely accepted and readily available. Talented MBAs can never have enough strategy frameworks or models. No matter which framework or approach is used, however, strategy formulation boils down to answering three simple questions:

1. What is our central purpose, and how will we create value?

2. What is our unique source of differentiation that will set us apart?

3. Where will we focus our attention, based on market opportunity?

These three questions provide what is almost a "paint by numbers" strategy development guide, similar to your child's first foray into the art world. Answering these questions will get you to a strategy, yes, but the quality of the strategy will depend on how well you "color between the lines" as you analyze the various options and make choices. If you get it right, the output will present a clear picture of the path forward.

Equally important to the quality of the strategy is a leadership team's *Execution IQ*. Execution IQ refers to the leadership team's ability to ask the right questions about what it will take to act with conviction and commitment to execute the strategy: Is this the right strategy for our organization, and how will we execute it? Execution IQ also refers to the capacity to assess and understand the organization's readiness and ability to execute strategy based on the suitability of the organization design and the quality of its talent (see Figure 3.1).

Our experience working with leaders in North America, Europe, and Asia is that Strategy IQ, or the tools and means to formulate strategy, has far outstripped Execution IQ, the capabilities and means to achieve strategic priorities

A quick inventory of the elements that make up Strategy IQ reveals that it leans heavily on the left-brain analytical activities associated with tasks like problem solving, data analysis, assessing trade-offs, and prioritizing (see Figure 3.2). The application of Strategy IQ helps leaders figure out the organization's purpose and how it plans to create value and sustain differentiation. In most organizations, strategy requires a refresh or confirmation, versus an overhaul every year; and once leaders establish how a company will create value, Excel spreadsheet models and their masters can go to

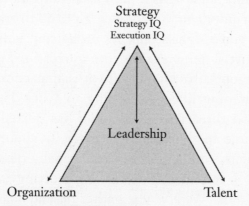

**Figure 3.1   The Shockproof Model**

| Key Elements of Strategy IQ | Key Elements of Execution IQ |
| --- | --- |
| Ability to . . . | Ability to . . . |
| • Define a purpose and plan an approach to create value. | • Understand the organization's readiness to execute the strategy. |
| • Analyze the competitive landscape and market conditions. | • Ensure that the capabilities, business processes, and structure are in place to support the strategy. |
| • Identify a unique source of competitive advantage. | • Create a talent strategy that defines the number, type, and quality of people needed and make sure they are effectively sourced and deployed. |
| • Select and prioritize areas of focus (markets and products). | • Dynamically adjust the connections between strategy, organization, and talent, as needed. |

**Figure 3.2   Strategy IQ and Execution IQ Elements**

work to figure out which combination of products, services, and markets will provide the best set of opportunities looking across the competitive landscape.

With effort and focus, Strategy IQ can be developed and refined. Take a look at Tellabs Inc., a company that provides communications service providers like AT&T and Verizon with the nuts and bolts that make networks work. The company's equipment is deployed globally to transmit data, video, and voice signals, and its broadband network access and transport systems enable communications providers to create fiber-optic backbone networks that connect incoming and outgoing lines. According to CFO Tim Wiggins, over the past three years leadership has started to invest a lot more time in thinking systematically about their markets, products, and organizational capabilities. "We have always had a very strong R&D, engineering, and product focus," he said. "We are now gathering and analyzing more data about the markets in which we operate, including their profit characteristics. We have become externally focused, and as a result understand much better what we *need* to do, and not just merely what we *can* do."[4]

Wiggins shared that Tellabs's leaders are "really digging deep to understand competitors and where we can reasonably win. This level of analysis is informing our strategic choices to a greater extent." In his view, this represents a very positive progression and is helping set the company firmly back on the right course after a challenging period. Tellabs is now investing a significant amount of its R&D effort into products that address the rapidly growing market for wireless Internet services, driven by users of smartphones and mobile computers. This strategy has been paying off. The company is seeing an increase in revenues from the sales of wireless data-centric products. Wiggins believes that, in the past, Tellabs relied on the commitment and determination of its people, and probably didn't spend enough time on analysis and reflection to get the strategy right. He recounts that, "We would set a direction and rely too heavily on our commitment to working harder than the next guys, even if the direction we chose was inherently limited by the size or scalability of the market opportunity."

Wiggins also stresses the importance of staying focused and taking care not to fall back into old habits. "Once we identified what needed to get done as part of our strategy, we developed an Executive Dashboard that tracked the most vital metrics and leading indicators around our priorities and strategic direction. Every two weeks, the executive team monitors and course-corrects progress toward our goals, ensuring that we never lose sight of the key imperatives we need to achieve in order to successfully execute our strategy."

Leaders in Shockproof companies exercise Strategy IQ, but they also demonstrate a bold and relentless commitment to Execution IQ. Many leaders believe that implementation occurs once strategy has been developed, which is tactically correct; but in a Shockproof company, Execution IQ figures prominently throughout the strategy development process, as well. When developing the strategy, leaders already have one eye on execution, and they are thinking through whether or not a strategy is right for their company, and how to execute it. However elegant the strategy might appear on paper, its true value is only realized if and when it is effectively executed. The Shockproof way is to first make sure the strategy is *not wrong*, and then to put the right organization and talent in place to successfully execute.

## ECONOMIC DOWNTURN PROVIDES JUICY OPPORTUNITY

Most of the business leaders with whom we have communicated during the 2008–2009 economic downturn have lamented the fact that the recession had stifled their growth plans, and they were anxiously awaiting their markets to rebound. Not so in the case of Edgar Huber, President of Juicy Couture, the contemporary fashion brand that designs clothing and accessories for young women and girls. Huber, with 15 years' experience building brands for consumer products powerhouses, took the reins at Juicy Couture in 2008 and has been steering the company in a new direction ever since. Huber describes the situation when he arrived at Juicy Couture as one that needed a major strategic and operational overhaul. "We had become too focused on distribution and meeting quarterly results, and as a result we were not doing the right things to support what truly is a great brand, one that consumers love."[5]

The recession stimulated the impetus for change, he emphasized. "It provided the shock to the system that the company needed and allowed me the opportunity to generate the type of change that might not have been possible otherwise." What quickly became apparent to Huber was that the focus on quarterly results—or, as he describes it, "mechanical growth"—wasn't sustainable and "certainly couldn't get the business to the billion-dollar mark that Liz Claiborne, the parent [company], envisioned for the brand." The company had become "so distribution and short-term results focused that it was stuffing the channels with product, versus tending to the brand." Looking through the Value Lens (introduced under "Shockproof Lenses," in Chapter 2), and thinking about what matters most in the fashion and apparel business, Huber concluded that, "Juicy Couture had simply lost sight of the need to manage the brand proactively."

Huber characterizes the process of making the strategic shift as "a time race against the recession." During his first month on the job in September 2008, he noted that "comparable store sales were down 10 percent, and the next 14 to 15 months were [going to be] equally challenging." He realized that the degree of strategic change required at the company was far-reaching and "went well beyond a minor change in strategy." Juicy Couture was a division of Liz Claiborne Inc., although, at the time was still being run by its founders. According to Huber, there was a great deal of entrepreneurial spirit associated with their continuing involvement, but "the business lacked the structures, systems, processes, and people required to create an engine for growth." He described the crux of the change in strategy this way: "We had a [clothing] collection that was designed and built for wholesale, and adjusted to meet the needs of retail stores. And now we have a collection that is designed for retail and adjusted for wholesale." Huber underscores that this new strategy is based on "moving from a wholesale and distribution focus to a retail and digital channel [Internet] focus." This strategic shift required upgrades to "the product design engine—and also talent, in some instances"—to make it happen, according to Huber.

It wasn't only the product engine that required significant redesign to support growth. Applying the Systems Lens, Huber realized that all the interconnected functions, processes, and talent required recalibration to align them with the new direction. Huber described the challenge: "We needed to rebuild and professionalize everything, from design, sales, and marketing to public relations, human resources, and finance." He also shared an interesting comparison, and some insight, between what's required at Juicy Couture and his experience managing brands in the cosmetics industry. He said, "In the cosmetic business, you provide your brand to the stores, set up product counters, train the staff, and then sell the product. The retailers have very little influence over the brand and how it is positioned." Emphasizing that differentiating Juicy apparel is key, he points out: "You provide the brand to the retailer, and if after one or two seasons the sales numbers slip, retailers are quick to diminish the brand's positioning in the store; the amount of space provided [shrinks], and pretty soon product ends up on hangers in the corner."

In the apparel business, Huber says, "You really need to control your brand and be much more hands-on at the retail level." While the process of setting the strategy required a good deal of analytical thinking and rigor, the sales data made it relatively easy for Huber to see what needed to happen. He invested a great deal of time and effort aligning senior leaders around the most critical capabilities necessary for Juicy Couture to execute effectively, and helping those leaders to focus on exactly what was required to reach the goal of becoming a billion-dollar brand. Making sure leaders are on the same page in regard to the key priorities, and looking at the business through a Value Lens to guide their actions, are important early steps in execution, according to Huber. Juicy Couture's leaders agreed that in order to realize its strategy, it was important to get closer to consumers and leverage consumer knowledge, drive creativity to improve the assortment of products, focus on retail productivity and e-commerce, expand internationally, and get the right talent in the right place. Huber stresses that, "Once everybody agrees on what's required to rebuild the brand, it becomes a lot easier to prioritize initiatives, allocate resources, and get people focused on doing the right things."

Once Juicy leaders were aligned on the direction, Huber and his team quickly planned the path forward. By applying the Change Lens, they figured out what adjustments were necessary to support the new direction and how to go about introducing the changes. This required a modification of the organization structure and several underlying core processes, from consumer research to design and sales. To get the right level of focus on the retail, wholesale, and Internet channels, he changed the structure, removed roles that formerly had multichannel responsibility, and opted instead for single-channel accountability. Huber also aligned the merchants by channel, to address the different needs and preferences of consumers in each one. He said that, "Getting closer to the consumer and understanding their needs to a much greater degree is critical to our success."

The level of retail expertise that Huber believes is absolutely necessary was lacking "all the way across the company, including in HR, so even the process of acquiring talent was difficult. Changing our strategy required a complete overhaul in how the company does business, all the way from design and innovation to decision making. The salespeople no longer decide what types of products to sell. It's the merchants who make those decisions now, and this is a big change. We need to know our customer. When you are selling to whole-sale, and you sell to Neiman Marcus, for example, they really know their customer. Now, we need to know our customer in each channel. That's the difference," he said.

Reflecting on the cultural change required to support the strategy, Huber commented, "The culture was one where people thought they could tell the consumer what they want, almost in an arrogant way. Now we have people who ask the question, 'For whom are we designing?' That's a shift. To get there, we needed to change out some of the people." Huber sees his role as one of "sustaining this new consciousness and culture that revolves around the consumer." People in the business needed to rethink their own roles and adapt to the new strategy and approach. "People had to completely change their mind-set. It was quite a shock moving from a distribution and wholesale model to a retail and digital chan-nel focus," said Huber.

The degree of change that Huber continues to drive at Juicy Couture requires both Strategy IQ and Execution IQ— although Huber places much more emphasis on the imple-mentation side of the equation. "To me, the nature and type of the strategic shift we needed was clear. Getting everybody else to not only see what's needed, but to fundamentally change their mind-set and put in place a new organization structure and processes is what's challenging." Huber also points out that while Juicy Couture was in the middle of this sweeping change, the brand still delivered a substantial amount of direct operat-ing profit to parent company Liz Claiborne.

## LEADERS WHO CREATE THE BATTLE PLAN CAN ADAPT THE BATTLE PLAN

In a Shockproof company, the strategy development process is greatly enhanced through genuine leadership collaboration. Harry J. Kraemer Jr., Executive Partner at Madison Dearborn Partners, and formerly Chairman and Chief Executive Officer of Baxter International Inc., a global leader in medical products and supplies, believes that getting the right level of engagement and reflection from leaders who are involved in strategy development is essential. "As a leader I would never recommend developing a strategy and then attempt to align others around it. The conversations between leaders that have a different perspective on the right way forward usually get you to a better answer."[6] Kraemer subscribes to the view that leaders need to apply their interpersonal skills to forge the types of trusting relationships that support frank, open, and honest dialogue and discussion about strategy. He also believes that Jim Collins got it right in his book *Good to Great* when he referenced the need to focus first on the "who," or making sure the "right leaders are on the bus," before turning attention to the "what," and setting strategic direction. "Making sure that the right leaders are on board and actively engaged is essential to success," Kraemer says. He asserts that it's "very helpful to have opposing points of view at the table during strategy sessions." Kraemer's perspective is that "if the right people are in the room, and they engage in balanced discussion, sharing of ideas, and analysis, the strategy will emerge and it will be one leaders can support."

Leaders in Shockproof companies are realistic about the fact that there will always be unknowns. They believe that the notion of a perfect strategy is a fallacy, as it contradicts the need for adaptability, flexibility, and opportunism. Kraemer maintains that business leaders can learn a lot from the military, especially when it comes to readiness to deal with the unexpected, the things that don't show up in the strategy document. "In business, by getting the strategy and values in place, communicating effectively, and having the right people, you have essentially planned for crises. No matter what occurs, you are ready to deal with it. People know what to do and how to respond." Military leaders, he says, demonstrate this preparedness and accept the need to be adaptable. They realize that battle plans are just plans. Contact with the enemy provides opportunity to test a strategy and make adjustments. In military training, scenario planning and routine exercises take the place of the enemy to achieve readiness. In business, Kraemer asserts that, "If the right leadership is in place, and they've worked together on the strategy, and share the same underlying values, when crises or unforeseen events occur, they can take a hit and respond effectively."

## BREAKING DOWN VERSUS BREAKING OUT

The common practice in strategy development is to "turn over every stone." Outside consultants are paid to do it. Legions of MBAs have perfected the art. The process usually involves breaking down every type of data and variable available and then analyzing, synthesizing, and packaging findings to clarify opportunities. While this makes good sense, it's only valuable as a starting point. Unfortunately, breaking down data and performing analytical gymnastics often become the focus, versus the means to stimulate thoughtful reflection and support sound decision making. Leaders need to achieve the right balance between breaking *down* and breaking *out*. Strategy work has become overly mechanical and analytical and is, therefore, often not reflective enough; that said, the process of developing strategy can be as valuable as the analytical output, if managed well.

Combining analysis with reflection, and data with imagination, can help leaders "break out" and unlock new ideas that depart from old ways of thinking. Asking the right types of questions can prompt leaders to think differently and, thereby, help raise Strategy IQ while also strengthening Execution IQ.

The types of questions we ask to promote reflection are:

- *Are we in it for the long haul?* To what extent does our strategy rely on a set of circumstances that may prevail in the short term, versus being a more durable, longer-term strategy?

- *Is what we do valued, and by whom?* If the company went out of business tomorrow, who would care most, and why?

- *Who is ready to fill our shoes?* How long would it take for a competitor to fill our shoes and provide the same value to customers if we exited the market?

- *Do over?* If we were starting over with a blank sheet of paper and the financial resources we have available to us today, what strategic choices would we make?

- *Do we believe?* To what extent does the strategy reflect each of our beliefs and assumptions as leaders about what's possible?

- *Are we committed?* Are we willing to make the changes we need to make, individually and collectively, to achieve our goals?

These questions prompt leaders to be more reflective and thoughtful. Avoiding the trap of creating a short-term strategy that's reactive in nature or designed to take advantage of a temporary condition in the market is important. Likewise, thinking in depth about how the business creates value, how it's differentiated, and what leaders would do differently if unencumbered by the current situation, whether positive or negative, can unlock new ideas. Getting a read on each leader's level of personal commitment to the strategy helps build alignment and gauges readiness for implementation.

The intent is to promote clear thinking and rich dialogue by accessing multiple perspectives and encouraging a level of engagement beyond what's usually achieved when relying on traditional strategy frameworks and analyses. The questions get to the heart of clarifying core capabilities. As the Juicy Couture example illustrates, reflecting on critical business value drivers and the internal capabilities needed to execute is just as important as the external analysis of the market and potential opportunities.

## STRATEGY IQ MEETS EXECUTION IQ

Before 2008, a loose grip, loose pocket change, or car keys could have a pretty devastating effect on mobile device screens. Recently, the common problem of a scratched, cracked, or shattered smartphone screen has been successfully addressed by a product (aptly named Gorilla glass) developed by Corning Incorporated's Specialty Division. The product is now steadily migrating its way from smartphones, laptops, and other mobile devices to television screens and other applications. At Corning's annual investor meeting in April 2010, CEO Wendell Weeks told shareholders that Gorilla glass has the potential to be a $1 billion or larger business within a few years.[7]

With over 150 years of materials science and process engineering under its belt, Corning Incorporated develops and makes keystone components that end up in a broad range of high-technology systems and products, from consumer electronics to emissions controls for automobiles, telecommunications, and life sciences. While Corning has a clear strategy, what's particularly interesting is the level of rigor the company applies to execution around its innovation, manufacturing, and commercialization processes.

Innovation at Corning Incorporated is serious business, as it should be, with 2009 revenues of $5.4 billion. Once the company decides to place a bet on an idea, a systematic governance process kicks in to oversee execution and coordinate the efforts of cross-functional teams. The governance process is made up of two distinct streams focused on coordination and decision making. The first is the Corporate Technology Council, led by Chief Technology Officer Joseph Miller, which is responsible for emerging or early-stage ideas. The second, the Growth and Strategy Council, is led by Corning Chairman and CEO Wendell Weeks and President and Chief Operating Officer Peter Volanakis; it kicks into gear when ideas are getting closer to commercialization. Amazingly, between February 2007 and May 2007, researchers at Corning dusted off a highly durable glass formula that had been developed 40 years ago and accelerated trials and research to arrive at a new solution that worked straight out of the gates. Such rapid cycle success is virtually unheard of with new glass composites. According to Abbie Liebman, the product line manager for Gorilla glass, "It's the fastest-moving project I've ever worked on."[8] Corning's strategy of developing keystone components for customer products and systems, combined with accelerated innovation and effective execution, delivered the prize.

While Gorilla glass revenues are growing at an impressive rate, due to strong demand, strategy refinement and implementation are also on the minds of Curt Weinstein and his team. Weinstein, a 24-year veteran of the company, is Vice President and General Manager, Advanced Optics, also in Corning's Specialty Materials Division. Weinstein and his team have been working steadily to refine their strategy, organization design, and operating model. Here's the challenge the team is addressing: Within the group are essentially four legacy businesses that bring together unique capabilities but were operating largely in silos. The businesses are highly diverse; they include ophthalmic applications, an aerospace and defense-focused business, and a semiconductor business that makes the mirrors and lenses that go into stepper machines used to etch designs onto silicon wafers. The business also has unique capabilities in metrology and thin-film coatings used in precision optical design.

With the global economy set back on its heels, "2008 and 2009 was a tough period for Corning's Advanced Optics, as the cyclical demand in the semiconductor industry was at the wrong end of a down cycle for our business,"[9] said Weinstein. "The impetus for change was the need to strengthen financial performance and create a more sustainable and resilient business. While we knew that our core capabilities and portfolio were not likely to change all that dramatically in the short term, we did have a sense that there were opportunities to bring together our unique capabilities in new and different ways to integrate them in more compelling and, frankly, more profitable ways." For example, the team believed that the aerospace and defense segment in which they operate "could potentially offer a 'less cyclical opportunity' that plays to our strengths."

Consistent with his personal leadership philosophy and style, Weinstein decided not to jump to the answer but instead to go through a structured process, to build leadership buy-in and commitment to the overall strategic direction. "This was particularly important to me given the fact that what we have here are businesses that are not only diverse in terms of capabilities but also have different cultures," he explained. The team embarked on several streams of analyses, including a detailed examination of the existing product portfolio and its relative profit and growth characteristics, as well as a value analysis to identify the drivers of success for the business. The analysis, according to Weinstein, was "particularly helpful in creating a fact base that confirmed what some of the team already knew intuitively, and what I was starting to see after a few months in the role."

Weinstein also reflected that, "It's in Corning's DNA to make decisions based on a strong fact base, so it made perfect sense for us to start with this foundation." The need for change became clear to him quickly. "It sort of jumps off the page when you see it all in one place. The numbers don't lie. Our situation wasn't sustainable financially so we needed to operate differently," he said. Leaders now agree on a strategy for Advanced Optics that is essentially capabilities driven. Integrating the capabilities more effectively will give Advanced Optics the opportunity to provide higher-value precision optical subsystems within their niche markets.

Gaining clarity on the strategic direction helped leaders to quickly coalesce around the need to manage and then deploy resources more efficiently, in every area from engineering and design through manufacturing and commercial management. "After all, unlike the other divisions in Corning, even the best of our opportunities is probably less than $100 million, due to the highly niche nature of what we do," said Weinstein, pointing out the need to better integrate existing capabilities and resources. Each of the legacy businesses recognizes the value that its counterparts provide in paving the way for increased collaboration, improved integration of capabilities, and a more structured go-to-market approach. The business is also run as a single P&L, instead of what was effectively a roll-up. Weinstein feels that, "Moving to a single P&L facilitates improved prioritization of initiatives and investments, cost reduction, and efficiency."

Interestingly, Corning's CEO Wendell Weeks ended his remarks at the 2010 annual shareholders conference by noting pragmatically, "We can't eliminate volatility from Corning's business, but it should be evident from our performance that we have built the company to survive difficult times, and we are committed to always living our values." Corning has certainly survived peaks and valleys, and it appears the company is as resilient as its Gorilla glass.

## MAKE SURE THE STRATEGY IS "NOT WRONG," AND MAKE IT STICK

Bob Irwin, CEO of Sterling Commerce prior to its acquisition by IBM in May 2010, has a strong conviction that while both are necessary, Execution IQ trumps Strategy IQ. In Irwin's case, of course, he started with his key mantra, "Making sure that the strategy is not wrong." At Sterling Commerce this translated into analyzing the key markets and industry verticals in which they operate and agreeing on a focused set of products. According to Irwin," The biggest learning I've had as CEO over the last three years is how incredibly hard it is to get everyone on the same page. What this points out to me is how important it really is to simplify the strategy. There are 24 hours in each day and 2,500 of us. The work unit is defined, and there is only so much that we can reasonably do. So let's make sure it's the right stuff," he said.

Irwin describes part of the challenge this way: "When you ask yourself the question, 'What should our strategy be?,' the opportunities are almost endless." His point is that if yours is a $50 to $100 billion company, the opportunities and scope for growth tend to be much narrower. Irwin believes that for companies of less than $1 billion in revenue that are already successful, figuring out exactly what the focus should be is more challenging. "What happens is that leaders say, we are already in order management and logistics management, so what's the next tangential product we should go after to get ourselves up to the $2 billion mark?"

By spending a lot of time focusing on these tangential or adjacent product opportunities, Irwin points out that, "We probably lost sight of what ultimately is a very simple set of facts. We have a 2 percent share in order management. So which is harder, getting from 2 percent to 10 percent in something that we already do, or getting to 2 percent in three other things that we don't do yet?" It was this kind of thinking that ultimately helped Irwin's leaders land on what turned out to be a pretty straightforward strategy. "We do six things really well, [have products] in five industries and in six countries. And, by the way, these products, in five industries and six countries, represent almost 90 percent of our revenues. There's the key to our strategy. Focus. Very simple. What's the likelihood that this strategy is perfect? Zero. What's the likelihood that it's wrong? Zero. Leaders waste way too much time trying to get the strategy to be perfect and not enough time implementing it."

What Irwin quickly realized, however, is that while it might be easy to declare the strategy or write it down, what's really hard is "getting 2,500 people to behave consistently with the strategy." The other way Irwin directed focus to the strategy was to reinforce that Sterling Commerce is a software products company. This was important in response to some tension, and questions by people in the business who thought Sterling Commerce should expand more into the professional services space, versus professional services simply being the means by which to implement the products.

Irwin demonstrates that he understands the dynamics of change and the reason all leaders need to use the Change Lens effectively. As he recalls, "It took us almost 18 months to get everybody to truly believe that this is our strategy." He described traveling to Sterling's offices in the United States and abroad during this time frame and seeing people work and become excited about opportunities and products that fall outside of what he now refers to as the "six, five, and six" that represent the products, industries, and countries that make up the strategy. Irwin has given a lot of thought to this phenomenon, to the point where he's developed a model, or framework—which he refers to as the "ladder of human dynamics"—to explain it. There are seven steps on the ladder: hear, listen, understand, BELIEVE, commit, engage, and change. Irwin describes it clearly within the context of his experience as CEO at Sterling Commerce and his efforts to embed the strategy.

"When you explain the strategy to somebody, they hear you but they don't really listen, the first time. After you've repeated the strategy a few times, they start to listen, but they don't yet understand fully. When they have listened for a while, they start to genuinely understand." What that really means, according to Irwin, is that they internalize it and ask, "What does this mean for me?" The pivotal point, he says, is getting people to believe. What he means is that it's the point at which people realize, "No kidding, this is our strategy!?" Only when they come to this realization can they commit; and when they commit, they start to really engage, he believes. It's only when people engage and change that they can lead others and drive change.

What's important about Irwin's perspective is his conviction that until you get people to truly *believe* that what's being described and communicated *is* the strategy, they are less likely to act in ways that align with it. He says people need to take time to absorb things and move from not listening to understanding and, finally, to believing. The problem in many companies, Irwin contends, is that "just about when people are getting ready to believe in the strategy, something changes." He continues: "Maybe the business has a bad quarter, or maybe even just a bad month. Or the leader attends a seminar about an emerging technology, or reads a recent economic report about a particular market, or there's an acquisition. Just then, when people are finally ready to change, the leader changes the strategy and people go all the way back to the first step."

This "flavor of the month" perception on the part of employees plays out in many organizations where leaders are inadvertently teaching people to "wait out" a particular strategy or leader and basically keep doing the things they were doing before the new strategy, even when these activities or initiatives are not connected to the new strategy and don't add value. Ascribing to Irwin's model of hear, listen, understand, BELIEVE, commit, engage, and change is a good way to stay focused on the level of effort required by leaders to get people pulling together to execute strategy.

## MAKING TECHNOLOGY MORE THAN AN AFTERTHOUGHT

Shockproof companies ensure tight alignment between business strategy and technology strategy. Why? Because technology can, in fact, be a key element of strategy, more so than an enabler of it, even when the company is not in the technology space. Virginia Gambale is a highly regarded technology expert who was voted one of the top three CIOs on Wall Street in 1997; she founded Azimuth Partners in 2003, an advisory services firm for technology companies seeking to grow, raise capital, and position themselves for significant transactions. Gambale has served on more than 20 private and public company boards and has cultivated a very keen sense for the role that technology can and should play in companies. In many companies outside the technology space, technology is often considered as an implementation tool that enables strategy. Not so at JetBlue Airways, says Gambale, who sits on JetBlue's board.

JetBlue Airways, according to Gambale, "competes for customer attention based on a combination of value, service, and style."[10] In 2009, the airline was ranked "Highest in Customer Satisfaction Among Low-Cost Carriers in North America" by J.D. Power and Associates.[11] Customers like the one class of service, the leather seats, decent legroom, and the array of amenities that include satellite TV and radio and movies. JetBlue has adopted several of the cost containment strategies of other low-cost carriers, such as bypassing airport lounges and full meal service. But where JetBlue departs from its competitors' models is that it operates more than one type of aircraft, believing that it can serve smaller markets more efficiently with smaller airplanes. Another key difference is that JetBlue creates competitive advantage through technology, versus simply using it to provide amenities on flights.

Gambale clearly applies the Systems Lens; she recognizes the need to constantly scan the external environment, customers, and the competitive landscape to inform strategy. She describes JetBlue's perspective on what's happening in the industry: "At JetBlue, we are very aware of the tremendous amount of consolidation that's taking place in the industry, but we have decided to remain independent. The larger players are consolidating and creating what they believe will be a competitive advantage by [building] the 'largest airline in the world,'" said Gambale. "We've had lots of opportunity to be acquired by the bigger players, but our feeling was that we have a product that is superior, we are a very specific niche player, and we serve a need in the industry, so we chose not to lose what we had created." What JetBlue did decide to do, however, was invest substantially in technology so that it could partner and form alliances with other airlines. "We had the foresight to say, ultimately, there's too much capacity in the industry. There is either going to be consolidation through acquisition; or, if other carriers recognize what we do best and want to partner with us, we need to make it easy to do. Technology investment became central to the strategy," Gambale explained.

To that end, JetBlue took on a significant multiyear project "to completely rebuild our reservation systems to create capabilities that allow us tremendous granularity in definition of product and service and the openness to partner with anybody," said Gambale. JetBlue's reservation system enables the company to price more legroom differently in one market versus another, or to charge different prices for a passenger who flies the airline once a year, or has never even flown or been a customer before. "Some of our competitors don't have a technology infrastructure that allows them to establish open partnerships," she said. Clearly, JetBlue views having the right technology in place as central to having a flexible, scalable model. "I think in order to be Shockproof in our industry, you need to have an open system capable of partnering with other airlines and adjusting your model as the industry develops," she adds. From a customer standpoint, the new reservation system offers a greater sense of choice, as customers can purchase multiple tickets at various levels of service and features, to match their preferences. The reservation system and the database behind it capture information about each customer's preferences and can reflect them by offering targeted options when the customer logs in next. It's a mass customization approach that connects the customer to the brand and to the airline's customer-centric strategy.

Technology is so pervasive in business today that it's critical that leaders ensure that the right technology strategy and infrastructure are in place to support growth, independent of industry or business model and regardless of organic or acquisitive growth. Virgina Gambale learned this in her days in financial services, and believes that too few senior executives understand this need, as evidenced by the fact that "so few public company boards have a technologist at the table, yet they end up taking massive write-offs for failed technology implementations," she said. Technology strategy needs to be, at the very least, integrated and aligned with business strategy if a business is to be truly Shockproof. In some cases, as with JetBlue, technology contributes to both the development and continual recalibration of business strategy, as opposed to being an afterthought or an implementation aid.

# KNOWING WHEN TO HIT REBOOT: EVERY STRATEGY HAS A SHELF LIFE

Shockproof companies also realize that the strategy that gets them to the top doesn't always keep them on top. It's just as important for leaders in companies that are winning to reflect and refine strategy as it is in companies that are struggling. In successful companies that achieve a solid run of financial performance and results, it's very easy to fall into a pattern of looking in the rearview mirror and calling for "more of the same." This is understandable, but not advisable. Leaders in companies that get caught flat-footed, basking in their success, routinely reflect on a culture that has a built-in reluctance to challenge the status quo or the established strategy. At IBM, for example, CEO Samuel Palmisano is willing to make bold moves by betting big on software and applications as a significant source of future growth and profit, instead of relying only on services as the engine to drive future growth. IBM is now pursuing acquisitions and strengthening internal capabilities to achieve its goals.

Dell is a great example of a company that achieved incredible success based on its unique strategy and competitive edge in operational execution. Going around the middle man and shipping direct to customers was a stroke of genius. But from the outside it appears that Dell became somewhat complacent and missed an opportunity to use its significant head start on the competition or the bundles of cash generated by its unique business model to fund an evolving strategy. The Dell story highlights the need for companies to think about their next growth platform and evolve their strategies when they're at the top of their game. Commenting in a 2007 *BusinessWeek* article on the challenges faced by Dell, Harvard Business School professor Clayton Christensen said, "When it's all you can do to keep up with the growth your current business model is providing, you just don't feel that urgency. It's hard to get worried."[12] Long-term sustainable growth demands reinvention—or, at the very least, evolution.

Since Michael Dell resumed the responsibilities of the top job in 2007, he has made multiple acquisitions, shed jobs, and closed factories. He also outsourced over 50 percent of production to reduce costs, and has continued the push to diversify beyond the company's core PC business, which still accounts for about half of revenues. In a talk at a June 4, 2010, Sanford C. Bernstein & Co. conference in New York, Dell said, "This transformation is incomplete. If I had to give it a grade, I'd give it an incomplete." He acknowledges that transformation at the required scale demands focus. "We're in the midst of a transformation and we're very focused on how we're doing in that,"[13] he said. It's also worth noting that Dell is still the third-ranking company in worldwide sales of PCs, behind Hewlett-Packard Development Co. and Acer Inc., so it's far from being caught in the inevitable downward spiral, as painted by some, but it does point to the need to continuously evolve strategy, especially when you're at the top.

## NOT WRONG, NOT PERFECT, BUT CLOSE ENOUGH

When leaders feel confident that their business strategy is close enough to being right without being *perfect*, they can put their energies into the work of strategy execution. It's then time to explore what organization and talent are needed to execute. That's where we will take you next.

# CHAPTER 4

# *Beyond Boxes and Lines*

All organizations are perfectly designed
to get the results they get.
—Arthur Jones

## Nurse, Scalpel Please

The period 2008 to 2009 was a tough one for many companies, as growth in the global economy hit the brakes and slowed to a crawl. It was an equally difficult period for employees, as well, especially for *former* employees. In Jason Reitman's movie *Up in the Air*, the George Clooney character, Ryan Bingham, is literally a high-flying professional who enjoys the trappings of airplane travel and his job as a "career transition" counselor. He flies all over the United States handing out pink slips to employees whose managers don't have the courage to pull the trigger themselves. The movie has a comedic tone, but it begins on a serious note, with a series of talking heads reflecting on their recent misfortune. And if they seem all too real, it's because *they are*. They aren't Hollywood actors, but real people, who had in fact been laid off across the United States during the 2008 recession.

Unfortunately, whether at the hands of a career transition specialist or, more humanely, an HR or line manager, this story has played out all too often in real life, across the globe, since 2008. Alarmingly, in 2009, the Fortune 500 alone shed 761,422 employees, through a combination of downsizing, spinoffs, and attrition.[1] Of course, in tough times layoffs are not an unexpected event, but their sheer volume, and the cold fact that the Fortune 500 experienced this level of job losses, is astonishing. Not to be ignored is another notable statistic: The Fortune 500 simultaneously notched up profit growth of 335 percent in 2009. Fifteen of the Fortune 500 companies accounted for approximately 390,000 of the total job losses, with Citigroup topping the charts at 57,700 or, an 18 percent reduction in staff, closely followed by Time Warner, with 56,000 job losses, representing 64 percent of its workforce. This begs another question: How can so many jobs be lost from big companies and yet they still manage to deliver their products or services? Is it possible they didn't have the right organization in place or the right approach to determine how many people they actually needed in the first place? Were they simply too fat and happy?

When you think about the word *organization* within the context of business, the first thing that comes to mind for many is the organization structure, usually represented by that all-too-familiar chart with the neatly cascading and connected boxes and lines. Given the economic conditions that we have weathered, it wouldn't be surprising if the word *organization* also conjures up an immediate association with reorganization, restructuring, and their unwelcome first cousin, the pink slip. Let's ponder a simple question to get right to the crux of the issue: *Why do organizations exist?* Answer: *Because we create them.* We create organizations to bring people with shared interests together in the pursuit of a common goal and purpose. Organizations and the people and processes that work within them help turn ideas into realities, and possibilities into products and services that create value.

Getting the right organization design in place increases the probability of effective execution. It's unthinkable that a general would lead troops into battle without first getting organized, by coordinating and connecting tactics and clarifying the roles and responsibilities of the soldiers to support a sound battle plan. In companies, it's people who collaborate on the corporate battlefield to implement strategies. Objectives such as desired brand positioning, market share, revenue growth, profitability, shareholder value, and sustainability are meant to contribute to defeating the "enemy." But with each additional objective, leaders are faced with the challenge of managing another layer of complexity.

Increased complexity in business is a fact of life as more and more companies are operating globally and dealing with geopolitical risk and the challenges of emerging markets. Technology has created both the opportunity and the necessity for companies to collaborate in new and faster ways. Additionally and importantly, the same growing complexity that exists in the external environment is also mirrored inside organizations, with myriad moving parts and functions—R&D, product development, procurement, manufacturing, distribution, sales and marketing, and customer service. You name it. Working in concert, the sky is the limit. Without effective communication and collaboration, however, the complexity can become an unspannable canyon.

Let's go a step further in exploring why organizations exist: *We create them so that we can implement strategy more efficiently and effectively*. If the organization design is getting in the way, leaders must change it. Bob Irwin, CEO of Sterling Commerce before it was acquired by IBM, is convinced that structure is less important than strategic clarity. "It's important to figure out how you go to market, but you can mess with the structure all day and it won't matter unless people are focused on the right things. If you believe people are smart, and I do, they can work around an imperfect structure. I'm not even sure there is such a thing as a perfect structure."[2]

Tim Wiggins, CFO at Tellabs agrees: "When we assessed our organizational effectiveness two years ago, we realized that most of our shortcomings boiled down to how we were making decisions. Consequently, we have made significant investments in organizational effectiveness that predominantly focus on our decision-making processes: We clarified who is making what decision; we started to strongly articulate our priorities; and we enhanced our ways of tracking and monitoring the execution of the decisions that were made. These investments continue to pay off more than our previous restructuring efforts."[3]

While it's tough for any organization to go through multiple rounds of restructuring, it's important that companies recover, learn from the experience, and move on. Consider Tellabs Inc., the supplier of critical equipment that supports the network infrastructure of global telecommunications providers. Tellabs has gone through a challenging series of reorganizations over recent years and has come out stronger and better positioned as a result. Wiggins smiled in response to the axiomatic statement: "All organizations are perfectly designed to get the results they get."[4] In his opinion, "Restructuring and layoffs are really a failure of management, to a certain extent. If you need to continually restructure, there comes a point when you have to ask yourself the question: *Have we really got the right game plan?*" As Wiggins reflected, "People always advise you to get the reorganization over with as quickly as possible. But in a down cycle or difficult period, it's often hard to know where the bottom is."

Wiggins, no stranger to turnarounds, likens the impact of several reorganizations to "a patient undergoing multiple surgeries." He takes the analogy further. "Eventually, scar tissue builds up, so focusing on recovery and getting healthy again after a series of layoffs is critical. It's important to get back on track and to make decisions that strengthen the company." In a strategic move in 2009, Tellabs Inc. made a $165 million acquisition of WiChorus. "Network capacity of our customers like AT&T and Verizon are being stretched by the demands of smartphones and what appears to be unrelenting consumer appetite for mobile data services," he said. The company's recent results are promising. First quarter 2010, net income was $45.9 million, up from $6.5 million in the first quarter of 2009. Tough decisions were followed by smart, growth-oriented investments, and it seems that Tellabs Inc. has turned the corner.

Seemingly, every time there's an announcement in the media about a CEO landing a new role, it's a safe bet it won't be too long before there's a follow-up story about a restructuring or reorganization at the direction of the new exec. Newly hired CEOs often "shake up" the leadership team and bring in a few trusted lieutenants. The thinking here is straightforward: They're ready-made allies. The accepted rationale is that they have a track record of success working together, and the CEO can count on them to move quickly. An early shake up signals decisiveness and can be a positive message for an impatient market. And since the most common reason a new CEO is hired in the first place is to bring about change and improve performance, why wouldn't he or she shake things up, and reorganize? Much of the time, what's also required is simplification. Effective CEOs have a knack for taking what's complex and simplifying the strategy. How often have we heard chief executives discuss the need to get "back to basics" or "back to our roots" when leading a turnaround?

The fact is, when companies struggle to execute strategy or deliver results, it's often not long until leaders turn their attention to the organization structure. A leader scrutinizing the organization chart might conclude that *we need to make decisions more quickly so let's take out a management layer*; or, *we need to be more closely aligned with our customers, so let's restructure around industry verticals*; or, since sometimes the focus is on achieving better teamwork across silos, *maybe we should move to a matrix structure?*

However, when looking at an organization chart, scalpel and pen in hand, the choices are relatively limited: trim out boxes, move the boxes around, add new boxes, change the names in the boxes, or draw some dotted lines. Too many leaders believe that changes to structure improve performance and deliver value. However, what usually changes when structure is modified are titles, pay, and reporting relationships. Changes to these aspects of organization design alone rarely lead to improvements in performance. Consider what happened at Chrysler LLC. It went through three reorganizations in a three-year period before going bankrupt and being combined with Fiat. Each time, in dizzying repetition, there were lots of promises and no results. Leaders are frequently too quick with the scalpel and the pen, and not just at Chrysler. A Bain and Company study conducted between 2000 and 2006 examined 57 reorganizations and found that less than "a third produced any meaningful improvement in performance."[5] Like cosmetic surgery, taking the scalpel to the organization chart is a quick fix. It might look better for a while, but it doesn't improve the health and well-being of the company from the inside out.

## SEEING BEYOND THE CHART

What an organization structure or chart can't do is depict the multidimensional layers of processes, activities, interactions, information flows, decision making, and talent that define how companies actually go about getting their work done. The static graphic of an organization chart doesn't promote the panoramic thinking required by leaders to identify all of the potential options to address a performance shortfall. Shockproof Organization Design encourages leaders to see organizations much more holistically, in an integrated way. When leaders go "beyond the chart"—the boxes and lines—they start to see important levels of connectivity between business processes, technology, and people.

Structure is rarely the driver of effective execution. In fact, it's usually the last item to attend to on the organization design punch list—unless of course, structure is the identified and agreed-on problem. A more integrated perspective can be applied to an entire company, a business unit, a function, a work area, or a team. Before you begin an enterprise-wide organization design, consider your strategy and how the company creates value.

## SHOCKPROOF ORGANIZATION DESIGN

Value and how it's created is the centerpiece of Shockproof Organization Design. The rationale is simple. The whole purpose of organization design is to improve strategy execution and, in so doing, create greater value. The key to getting it right is to ensure that all six elements depicted in Figure 4.1 are aligned and focused on creating value. For private companies, the primary financial measures of value are growth and profitability. Public companies focus on these measures, as well, and also try to maximize total return to shareholders. Shockproof companies pay attention to the financial measures, but they also cast a broader net when thinking about the measures that represent value. They think about value created for customers, employees, and the communities in which they operate. They also consider their environmental impact. On occasion, the link between a company's financial well-being and its environmental impact comes into very clear focus. As of early June 2010, British Petroleum's market capitalization had been reduced 55 percent as investors reacted to

**Figure 4.1   Design Elements of a Shockproof Organization**

the impact and fallout from the Deepwater Horizon oil spill that began in the Gulf of Mexico in April.[6]

Applying the Shockproof Organization Design approach requires leaders to test the integrity of each component of the organization design. Leaders should also confirm that the elements are appropriately integrated, so that the organization design enables the business to execute its strategy and create value. Changes to one element typically cause ripple effects, which need to be carefully managed. For example, changes to how work gets done typically lead to shifts in roles, accountabilities, and even the performance measures used to track and monitor effectiveness. Not every organization design effort requires an overhaul of all six elements, however. Sometimes all that's needed is a tweak to performance measures or roles and accountabilities, or a clarification of the interactions and decisions that support how to best execute the work. To illustrate how this works, let's take a quick look at the questions leaders must address to ensure that organization design supports strategy and is linked directly to how the company creates value.

1. *Work:* Is the organization clear about the work that needs to get done to create value, and the best way to get the work done? Answering this question clarifies both *what* work needs to get done and *how* the work will be done.

2. *Roles and Accountabilities:* Are the roles and account-abilities necessary to do the work clearly defined? If not, expect some things to fall through the cracks, and be prepared for the turf battles that ensue when multiple groups or people believe they are responsible for the same things.

3. *Performance Measures:* Are the right performance measures in place to guide, monitor, and assess execution effectiveness? Remember, "what gets measured gets done," and plan accordingly.

4. *Interactions and Decisions:* Are the interactions and decision rights that support oversight and execution of the work well defined? You may be clear on what these are, but if others don't have the same clarity, be prepared for a long line at your door.

5. *Stewardship and Governance:* Are the right processes in place to allocate resources appropriately, ensure alignment with company values and priorities, and maintain checks and balances?

6. *Organization Structure:* Is the right structure in place to provide management oversight and efficient execution of the work? Form follows function, meaning that the structure should support how the work is executed.

## AN EARLY WARNING SIGN TRIGGERS SIGNIFICANT ORGANIZATIONAL CHANGE

University life in the United Kingdom is not much different from the United States. For a start, university degrees are becoming less affordable in the United Kingdom and many students will expect to graduate with the sizable debt burdens that are all too common in the American system. Soccer and rugby replace college football and basketball as the focal events for the student body. But one experience that students on both sides of the Atlantic have in common is the ritual of leaving home in their late teens and, for the first time, finding somewhere to live independently. In the United States, accommodations provided by the schools and privately rented housing represent the bulk of student living options, while in the United Kingdom, privately rented housing is more common than accommodations provided by schools.

In the United Kingdom the largest and most reputable provider of student accommodation is UNITE Group Plc. UNITE Group, first listed on the London Stock Exchange in 2000, is an FTSE 250 company that provides living accommodations to 39,500 students in 132 properties across 24 towns and cities. UNITE's success and growth has been fueled by a focus on creating a superior living experience for its customers through a business model that leaders have carefully evolved over time, in line with the company's strategy and changing market conditions.

Initially, UNITE developed, owned, and managed all of the assets on its balance sheet. Financing was sought through debt (bond issuance and bank lending) and equity offerings in the public market. This approach worked well, and followed a traditional entrepreneurial operating model in the real estate sector. "We found sites, developed properties, and rented them, moving on to the next one," explained UNITE's

CEO, Mark Allan. The model worked just fine," he said, "until we experienced an early warning about the fragility of our financing model."[7] This "early warning" occurred in 2001, when UNITE's capital-raising efforts coincided with the dot-com crash and the terrorist attacks of 9/11, making access to capital very challenging. It was the first sign that UNITE might need to "reconsider how growth was financed and how the business was organized, operated, and led," said Allan. Leaders started thinking long and hard about how UNITE creates value, and the criticality of ensuring access to capital while also refining its operations and internal processes to support scalable, profitable growth.

In 2003 and 2004, UNITE's executive leadership accelerated the conversations that would take them to where they are today. They applied the Systems Lens to "analyze the economic environment, the competitive landscape, and the implications for our business model, and our internal infrastructure, operations, and processes," said Allan. They concluded "that the substantial leverage on their balance sheet presented a risk to their growth plans, and that significant investment was required to improve organization effectiveness." This initiated a series of sale-leasebacks and joint ventures, and moved ownership of properties off UNITE's balance sheet. The deleveraging of the balance sheet would help position UNITE for the big shock to come: the "great recession."

In addition, according to Allan, UNITE's leaders recognized that the "student accommodation sector has many characteristics that appeal to investors— it's noncyclical in nature and demographic trends indicate that student numbers are rising, occupancy rates are high, cash flow is very predictable, and there is a structural supply-and-demand imbalance." This set of characteristics gave management the insight and confidence to set up a unique dedicated sector fund, UNITE UK Student Accommodation Fund (USAF). The fund offers institutional investors an opportunity to coinvest in a multi-investor fund, while providing UNITE with a means to access capital and free up cash for growth, as it sells partial ownership of properties it develops to the fund. The fund had approximately £1 billion ($1.5 billion) as of May 2010.

When the global financial crisis hit, many similar businesses collapsed under the weight of too much debt, but not UNITE. Its reaction to the earlier shock in 2001 had insulated its balance sheet from destabilizing leverage and put the company in a position to focus on evolving its operations and achieving scalable growth. The property management business and its operations went "through significant cost reduction of the order of 20 percent to reach desired levels of efficiency and profitability, while maintaining the high levels of customer service associated with our brand,"[8] according to UNITE's Chief Operating Officer, John Tonkiss.

The transformation at UNITE was a lot broader and deeper than getting the financing aspect of the business right. Leaders at the company used the Value Lens to focus their organizational design improvement efforts in the areas that would have the greatest positive effect on the business. They used a *value tree mapping* process to clarify the linkages between the capabilities and processes that support strategy execution and, ultimately, drive value. Leaders examined the work that needed to get done to execute the strategy, and concluded that financing, developing properties, and managing properties were really three separate but related capabilities that should each be organized as such, and operated for maximum returns. This insight caused UNITE's leaders to realize that they needed to change how the organization was designed and managed, to optimize results. They carefully considered how much change the business could absorb and, subsequently, how to involve as many layers of the organization as possible at the right time and at the appropriate level of detail.

UNITE management not only understands how their business creates economic value, they are also very deliberate about creating a positive impact in the communities in which they operate. For example, they focus on urban regeneration and run a carbon management program in conjunction with the United Kingdom's Carbon Trust. They incorporate renewable energy into their building design and promote the use of furnishings and products from sustainable sources. UNITE also leverages modular construction methods that use 30 percent fewer materials by weight, reducing transportation costs and carbon emissions, as well as the amount of waste generated at construction sites.

UNITE leadership didn't start transforming the way they work, go to market, and deliver value to customers by reviewing the organization chart. Instead, they started exploring and understanding in great detail the essential work required to execute their strategy. This approach included refining key work processes and operations "to build a highly professional property management operation," said Allan. The team identified and agreed on the core operational capability requirements to deliver accommodations and services, and made substantial investments in, for example, a technology infrastructure to facilitate online renting of UNITE's properties. Finally, management initiated a customer service center to support the operation. According to UNITE's COO, John Tonkiss, many roles in the business needed to be redesigned to align responsibilities and activities with the charge—"customer-led, city-driven, and profitable."

Leaders gave incumbents in UNITE's Operations Manager role increased responsibility and greater decision latitude. Operations Managers, the nerve center of the business, were identified as strategic or pivotal roles. They ensure that everything runs smoothly, by managing the consistent and effective execution of the redesigned work processes. The Operations Manager role is, in many ways, a steward of UNITE's customer value proposition. According to Tonkiss, "We introduced new performance measures in each area of the business," to monitor what was most important and to drive greater accountability for results. To close the loop, UNITE introduced a new corporate governance and leadership operating model, to ensure capital allocation and investment decisions supported the strategy and to oversee efficient operations. According to Allan, "The entire organization redesign was intended to ensure steadfast focus on UNITE's unique selling proposition and leverage its operational property management expertise." Added Tonkiss, "Managers need to have the right level of process in place to guide their efforts but still retain the flexibility to react as challenges arise and opportunities present themselves in their cities. We knew the changes we were making were significant so we invested a lot of time communicating with our people, making sure that they understood the new direction." Leaders at UNITE tackled each of the elements of organization design and ensured that the work, roles, performance measures, decisions rights, governance, and organization structure were aligned with creating value and integrated effectively.

Both Allan and Tonkiss reference the importance of the Change Lens. They recognize that managing such an organizational design change is "not an event but a process, a dynamic work in progress," with the biggest payoffs likely still ahead.

## WHAT'S THE WORK THAT NEEDS TO GET DONE?

When Jesse Cates, Shared Services Division Vice President at Corning Incorporated was tapped on the shoulder in 2004 and asked if he would take on a new challenge to build his organization, he jumped in, feet first. After all, he was the right guy for the job, although on the surface it might not have seemed so. He had no experience running shared services. A successful manufacturing leader, he had never remotely considered shared services as a career option, and didn't know where to start. What he did know, however, was perhaps more valuable: He knew where *not to start*. Instead of starting with a blank piece of paper and trying to draw an organization chart, he asked a series of questions to help him decipher the task ahead. The first questions Cates asked were, "What's the size of the task, and what would success look like?"[9] In 2001, Corning's expenditure on corporate staff functions, including Finance, IT, HR, and Procurement, hovered at around 10 percent of its $3.7 billion in revenue. At this point in time, Shared Services was in its infancy stage at Corning.

Armed with the data on the "size of the prize" and the task ahead, Cates went about the challenge in typical Corning fashion. The next set of questions Cates asked are those Corning leaders, managers, and researchers ask every day when attempting to solve complex component design issues for customers. Instead of taking a more conventional approach, Cates started to think through the core capabilities that would need to be integrated and the work that would be required to deliver shared services. He sidestepped the typical temptation to "immediately fill his own personal knowledge gaps in key support staff functions by loading up with CPAs, HR specialists, IT experts, and Procurement people," he said. Instead, he built a capability-based organization.

Cates reached back into Corning's divisions and hired Electrical Engineers and Manufacturing Process Engineers. He later added functional specialists, but that's not where he started. He remembers: "In every division and at every manufacturing facility, and in our R&D center, the same things were happening every month. Every month we needed to close the books. Every month employees were being paid. The real opportunity was in the fact that everyone was doing things their own way." The rationale for hiring Manufacturing Engineers is easily explained by Cates: "These are people who understand processes. They get the meaning of inputs and outputs better than most. They have spent their entire careers focused on refining processes and removing variation. They come to the table with problem-solving skills, tools, and methodologies like Six Sigma that can be directly applied." Cates's thinking reflects an ability to simplify and ask the right questions when approaching organization design. What work needs to get done? What capabilities are needed to do it? What organization will support getting the work done?

Cates and his team applied the Value Lens and turned their attention to thinking through how Shared Services could add value and how to design the organization. He began to reflect on his experience as a manufacturing leader in his previous roles. "I quickly realized," he said, "that I enjoyed the challenge of complex manufacturing tasks. I enjoyed working with engineering and design and applying manufacturing excellence principles. What I enjoyed less was making sure we closed the books on time each month and dealing with issues related to payroll problems and procurement and IT challenges." The goal for Cates and his Shared Services organization has always been to reduce transactional work in the divisions, allowing them to focus on what they do best.

Cates takes a very pragmatic view: "These guys are innovating and inventing. They are coming up with completely new ways to integrate capabilities. What we're doing here is defining and refining processes while emphasizing a performance focus, with the goal of nothing less than world-class execution and performance."

Demonstrating the use of the Change Lens, Cates put himself in the shoes of his customers; shoes he had worn before in his 22 years at Corning. He remembered his previous roles and that he "liked having control over things that could influence his performance and results." If inventory was being mismanaged, and not enough material was available to meet the schedule, "I knew exactly who to go to. They worked for me," he said. At Corning, division vice presidents are held accountable for results. Culturally and historically, division leaders liked to have control of staff functions, making this a delicate cultural shift to implement. As he puts it, "We had to prove ourselves. We had to earn trust through demonstrated success. It took time, but we now are well positioned." The change associated with asking division leaders to give up control of business support functions was carefully managed by the Shared Services team.

Cates and his team spent time making sure all employees were clear about their roles and responsibilities. They also introduced a dashboard with a balanced set of performance measures that capture service delivery quality, process quality, productivity, cost-to-serve, and customer satisfaction. "We use the performance measures very actively, to make sure we are delivering at targeted levels and to get the entire team focusing their efforts on what really counts. We regularly make changes to how we are managing and executing work, based on the indicators," said Cates.

Today, Corning's Shared Services Division has 250 employees, located across the United States, Asia, and Europe. Their track record is impressive; they have reached a 4 to 4.5 Sigma performance level, as benchmarked externally by the Hackett Group using Six Sigma. "Six is the target; but it's a journey," said Cates. Aggressive cost reduction goals continue to be set. "What started as a *push* to get the businesses to use our services is evolving to a *pull*," he explained. And as Corning's Shared Services prepared to expand its order management supply chain offering in 2010, it's no surprise that Jesse Cates was, "determined to start with *the work*," as he put it. "I've learned from experience that if we start with the work, the right structure will follow." Cates and his team believe that Corning's decision to build its own shared services capability is saving the company over $30 million annually, compared to fully outsourcing the operations.

## TRADING UP

James McNulty knows a thing or two about financial markets and driving strategic transformation to create value. He is Chairman of the Board of NYSE Liffe U.S., the futures exchange arm of the New York Stock Exchange. McNulty served as President and CEO of the Chicago Mercantile Exchange (CME), the world's largest futures and options exchange from 2000 to 2003, steering CME to a successful initial public offering (IPO) in 2002. The CME had previously been a member-owned not-for-profit that demutualized in 2000 after an overwhelming majority of members who owned seats at the exchange voted to take it public.

The strategy was always clear in McNulty's mind. What was challenging was the degree of organizational change required in regard to how the CME was organized and led during, up to, and after the IPO. "The members had voted clearly for the change, so what was on my mind was figuring out how to make it happen, which is why I was brought in as CEO."[10] Reflecting on the significance of the change, and oversimplifying for effect, McNulty describes the shift this way: "One day the members were players at the table in a casino and the next day they owned the casino. Their priorities began to change."

Members who previously focused on "maximizing their own day-to-day profits needed to change their mind-set," said McNulty. "We needed people to think very differently about how the organization creates value." He immediately set his focus on "building alignment around how the CME would create long-term value for its shareholders," he said. Getting everyone in "agreement about what we wanted our vision, mission, and values to be took time—almost two years," he added. Taking a page out of the playbook of Cisco's John Chambers, he had card-sized vision, mission, and values statements laminated and distributed to employees, to carry around with their CME identification badges.

McNulty "recognized the need for a common language and performance framework that leaders, the Board, and all CME employees could rally around," to drive shareholder value and to ensure appropriate governance. He introduced the Gordon-Shapiro growth model as the centerpiece of his transformation and alignment efforts and to ensure appropriate governance and stewardship. The model provided a means to explain value creation to employees and guide the activities and efforts of management and the Board. McNulty said his "goal was to make sure that every single employee understood [his or her] role in creating value by hitting budget goals, keeping down the cost of equity through risk management, and creating growth in free cash flow through innovation in product and process. This focus extended all the way from the Board to the guy who polishes the brass on the front door handles of the building." McNulty also made sure that "roles and responsibilities and performance expectations were clear, and reflected in the performance management process."

In addition, McNulty leveraged technology by moving the CME foreign exchange, equity, and interest rate products onto a greatly improved electronic platform and accelerating the expansion of the CME's global footprint. The CME also went through a process to professionalize several of its functions, from Human Resources to IT and Finance, in preparation for making the CME a public company. During McNulty's tenure, the exchange also "introduced a new structure and performance management system, to drive greater accountability." When the CME went public, members and shareholders benefited significantly from the preceding years' transformation efforts orchestrated by McNulty and his team. The initial public offering raised $166.3 million, and the CME had set the stage for how to take a major U.S. financial exchange public, and succeed. McNulty believes that the keys to successfully transforming the CME were: creating a common understanding of value creation; a governance and performance framework; and leadership practices that set clear objectives and held people accountable for delivering results.

In the preceding three examples, leaders designed their organizations around value creation. The necessary work to execute strategy was defined, roles and accountabilities were clarified, and the right performance measures were put in place. Decision boundaries, governance practices and processes, and the right organization structure were created to support the strategy. These are core elements of Shockproof Organization Design.

## DIAGNOSING ORGANIZATION DESIGN ISSUES THE SHOCKPROOF WAY

As a leader, the next time you assess barriers to strategy execution in your business avoid the temptation to simply change the organization structure. Instead, go "beyond the boxes and lines" and use a comprehensive diagnostic approach to ensure that the organization design that you build is Shockproof and supports efficient strategy execution. When you are thinking about changing organization design we encourage you to consider the following organization design insights.

### *Take the Time to Unwind*

It's rare that a company, function, or department has the opportunity to start from a blank sheet of paper. Most organizations have a defined structure, business processes, and ways of getting work done. The way a company operates at any one point in time tends to be a reflection of multiple layers of design decisions that have been made over several years and, frequently, by different leaders. For example, at one point a company may have organized its resources to align with the industry verticals it serves; alternatively, it may have been organized around product or service offerings. When a new leader joins a company, he or she often resets the direction, based on an analysis of the situation. Additionally, as strategy changes or evolves, changes to the organization occur.

As a result, the old ways of organizing and executing work, and often the technologies that support the business, never get fully unwound prior to the implementation of the new design. Remnants of various design decisions are layered on top of each other, are difficult to change, and tend to stick around even when they are no longer viable. When Tellabs's CFO Tim Wiggins talks about "scar tissue" remaining after corporate reorganizations, he is referring to old ways of doing work that no longer align with new strategy. Similar to plaque building up over time in the arteries of the heart, the legacy business processes and ways of working accumulate on top of one another in companies and lead to a constriction in the effectiveness of key business processes—a virtual clogging of the corporate arteries. At UNITE Group Plc, leaders stepped back and unwound several layers of previous processes prior to layering in new ones, as did Jim McNulty when transforming the Chicago Mercantile Exchange. In Shockproof Organization Design, leaders "take the time to unwind" and fearlessly tackle thorny legacy organization design issues.

## Try Looking from the Outside In

Let's assume for a moment that a company is located at one site, in a single building. Imagine lifting the roof off the building and looking top down at the CEO, his or her direct reports, and only peering at the subsequent layers below, all the way to the frontline employees. That's not unlike looking at an organization chart. You see organized layers, top to bottom.

What's far more insightful is to consider looking from the *outside in*, as if through a side wall of the same building, and thinking about how all the various layers, functions, people, and processes interact to create products and services that deliver value to customers. Standing in the customers' shoes and tracing a product back through the organization often uncovers both the bottlenecks and opportunities for improvement to strategy execution.

## Respect the "Emotional Chart," but Don't Be a Slave to It

The point here is that the organization chart is a highly sensitive and emotionally charged topic. Why? People's names are in the boxes. They have worked hard, often most of their careers, to secure their spots on the chart. Their investment in college education at prestigious schools "prepared them for this moment," not to mention the sweat equity and time on the job they've invested to get to where they are. Also, don't underestimate the weight of the work/life balance trade-offs that people make. Missing a son or daughter's first soccer game or school play to work on a project with a tight deadline is often seen as an "investment" in one's career, and a sign of dedication.

An employee's spot on the chart is typically tied to a menu of rewards, such as salary, bonus, and car allowance. The fact that real people are affected by the decisions made about organization structure is reason enough to begin the work of organization design far away from the organization chart and structure. This is why it is helpful to start organization design work with questions about how the company creates value and the work that needs to get done to deliver value, rather than starting with the organization chart. Frequently, the leaders directly involved in organization redesign initiatives have a vested interest in the outcome. Their immediate inclination is to secure their own place on the chart, instead of stepping back and asking a series of questions that ultimately help identify the best organization design to execute the strategy.

## Rome Wasn't Built in a Day

Thinking back on the evolution of UNITE's business and organization design changes, CEO Mark Allan shared that the most challenging aspect of leading this change was having patience. Both Allan and COO John Tonkiss demonstrated application of the Self-Awareness Lens, recognizing their own need for speed in executing strategy. "John and I had a very clear picture in our heads about where we wanted to get to, but we realized that getting 1,000 people to share that picture doesn't happen overnight," said Allan. According to Tonkiss, "Part of the challenge was the tension between knowing what we wanted to do and recognizing that we wouldn't get to a perfect answer a week from Tuesday. In fact, it may never be perfect. However, the steps we are taking now, and the outcome, will be so much more powerful when everyone in the organization is aligned and understands how they fit in."

Clearly, UNITE is getting it right. It has a portfolio under development and management worth approximately £2.5 billion ($2.75 billion) on completion; and the USAF fund that UNITE manages, and in which it has a significant minority stake, is at £1 billion ($1.5 billion).

Our perspective is that patience is important and that organizational change needs to be paced appropriately. Rome, after all wasn't built in a day and the Romans had a very simple organization chart!

## Not All Work Is Created Equal

Certain types of work and positions in a company have a greater level of influence on strategy execution and results. This is worth considering as you think about your organization design. Identifying the work that is most important, and making sure that it is designed effectively first, can have significant impact. Also, remember that the type of work that adds the greatest value isn't necessarily tied to the hierarchy in

BEYOND BOXES AND LINES

the organization chart. Work can be segmented into *strategic*, *core*, and *requisite* categories.

- *Strategic work* adds long-term competitive advantage to the company.

- *Core work* is central to a company's ability to deliver its products and services.

- *Requisite work* is work that needs to get done but has less value and may be addressed through an alternate resource model.

At UNITE Group Plc, the Operations Manager position was identified as *strategic*. This makes perfect sense, as an Operations Manager is responsible for overseeing how well all of the properties in his or her particular territory are managed; as such, an Operations Manager is at the front line, managing the UNITE brand and has a major influence on financial results and customer satisfaction. In companies like FedEx, UPS, or DHL, operations roles, central to getting packages from point A to B, might be considered strategic, as well. Knowing which work is most valuable and strategic can help focus organization design efforts, and also help prioritize investments in initiatives and talent.

If you have lived through a downsizing and were instructed "to make cuts from areas where it won't hurt us," or deliver a 10 percent headcount reduction across functions, you probably don't want to repeat the experience. Understanding the relative value and impact of the different types of work in the organization, can serve as a useful framework for making tough calls. Headcount cuts across the board run the risk of eroding competitive advantage, especially when they impact functions, jobs, or people that are responsible for executing strategic work.

## Be Careful What You Measure

What you measure gets the attention of others. What you pay for gets their undivided attention. Getting the right performance measures in place is critical to driving accountability and alignment. Tying different functions to a shared set of measures can help break down silos and foster the right types of conversations across teams. As CEO of the Chicago Mercantile Exchange, Jim McNulty used performance measurement as a centerpiece of the transformation effort, by introducing the Gordon-Shapiro growth model to focus efforts from top to bottom in the organization. It's important that one performance measure is not overemphasized at the expense of another. For example, most people would agree that productivity and quality and cost are all important, but how targets are set can have a real impact on the people doing the work. Recently, a group of call center employees participating in a focus group shared with us that they were cutting customer calls short and offering to call people right back to meet an overly aggressive average call-handling time target. The company preached quality customer service but managed the call-handle time target too stringently. The employee response, hanging up on customers and then calling them back so that all calls were recorded as being under the three-minute target, made productivity look good but severely damaged customer service.

Effective organization design includes a focus on establishing a balanced set of performance measures, not just financial results. Performance measures that monitor customer satisfaction or operational effectiveness may not delight Wall Street in the current financial quarter, but they tend to provide insight into whether a company will be around a few years into the future.

## Know Where the Buck Stops

The white space in between the boxes and lines of the organization chart is probably the area that companies pay the least attention to. Yet when decision boundaries are unclear, this white space can really tangle up execution, suck up time, and dilute results. When a function or a team has control over a process or activity, it usually gets done. When multiple teams or functions touch a process, and there is any lack of certainty around who has ultimate decision-making rights and who should be consulted to provide input, the gears can grind to a halt. New product introduction, for example, is a notoriously challenging process, as several functions touch it. At UNITE Group, leaders took a deliberate approach to list all the key decisions that typically get made, who owns the decisions, how and when decisions get made, and who should be consulted prior to making decisions. Speed and quality of decision making and the fact that decisions are supported, versus continuously challenged, is the prize for getting it right.

## Checks and Balances

If recent history in financial services and deep-sea oil drilling is any indicator, companies continue to struggle with governance and stewardship of resources. With the unprecedented level of pressure on leaders today to deliver short-term results, it's important to put "guard rails," or defined practices and processes, in place, to ensure leaders don't take on unnecessary risk, stray from the company's mission and values, or violate industry regulations. This is where the role of the Board in public companies comes into play. Tom Moran, of executive search firm Heidrick & Struggles believes that Boards today are "demanding that CEOs not only understand the businesses they lead but also have the underlying personal values and integrity to ensure that the company is operating consistently with its agreed-upon governance principles—it's a moral compass issue, as much as business acumen requirement."[11] Being Shockproof, by definition, requires that companies think through and carefully define stewardship and governance practices to avoid the risk that poor decision making by leaders will have a negative impact on stakeholders, including shareholders, customers, employees, and the communities in which the companies operate.

Remember, organization design supports strategy execution; but, ultimately, people implement strategy. The quality of talent in the business really matters. How effectively talent is acquired, deployed, developed, and rewarded is a foundational element of Shockproof companies. Let's look next at how businesses that are serious about becoming Shockproof think about their talent, the people they hire and deploy to execute strategy and deliver results.

# CHAPTER 5

# *Carbon Paper? Really?!*

There is no substitute for talent. Industry
and all its virtues are of no avail.
—Aldous Huxley

Peter Drucker. Michael Porter. Jim Collins. Malcolm Gladwell. Dilbert. *Dilbert?* Why would we add to such illustrious company Scott Adams's comic creation, the hapless, cube-dwelling techie who suffers dysfunctional coworkers, an evil feline Human Resources Director, and an inept boss? Like these gurus of management thinking, Dilbert is able to distill complex issues into simple truths through stories. Case in point is a memorable 1993 comic strip where Dilbert's boss tells his employees that though for years he had been saying that employees are his company's most valuable asset, "It turns out I was wrong." He continues, "Money is our most valuable asset. Employees are ninth." The real punch line? Carbon paper came in eighth.[1]

Funny? Yes. Sad? Yes—because it speaks to how valuing talent is at risk of becoming a cliché. It is true that for years employers everywhere have been touting their people as their "most valuable asset," but how many have meant it? More to the point, how many have acted accordingly? In fact, the claim has been repeated so often in some cases as to render it meaningless to employees who know better and respond with smirks rather than smiles to a declaration they know to be baseless. But all hope is not lost.

An interesting—and predictable—shift in management thinking took place around the time Dilbert's boss was having his revelatory moment. Fueled by blistering economic growth and the aging of baby boomers throughout the workforce, mainstream management thinkers began to come to terms with the idea that people *are* essential to the success of their employers. Whether through academic studies, anecdotal observation, or simply by applying common sense and the principles of supply and demand, organizations actually began to notice the role talent played in their success. Regardless, it's what we like to refer to as one more stunning example of a *blinding flash of the obvious.*

This is not to say that we can't point to examples of leaders and businesses that have talked the talk and walked the walk to success. The poster child for making talent a priority is GE's legendary CEO Jack Welch, who regularly preached *and* practiced the importance of hiring outstanding people and helping them develop to the fullest of their potential. As Welch said to an American Bankers Association conference in 2006, "This whole game is about talent—whoever fields the best team wins. Nothing you do is as important as building talent."[2]

And so, faced with mounting evidence, organizations and their leaders have begun to make it a priority to attract, retain, develop, and motivate the best people they can find. Corporate Staffing Managers are now Vice Presidents of Talent Management, Recruiters are Talent Acquisition Specialists. Personnel Representatives who had focused on pushing paper were upgraded to Human Resources Business Partners to the line organizations they supported. Even the slow-to-change federal government has gotten into the act by creating the role of Chief Human Capital Officer, to lead its efforts at the agency level. This tidal wave of change represents more than just the renaming of departments and retitling of roles. It speaks to a massive and important move toward the management of human capital with the same rigor, attention, and care as has traditionally been accorded to financial capital.

While numerous organizations have made this transition, many have realized that hiring, developing, and retaining the best and brightest is not enough. In the wrong roles, or misaligned with strategy, talented people have the potential to become disenfranchised or even a barrier to enduring success. Consider the company synonymous with the photocopier: Xerox. Because its leaders had become smitten by the success of technology leaders like Microsoft, Intel, and scores of Silicon Valley start-ups during the 1990s, Xerox embarked on a campaign to hire the best engineering talent to drive innovation in its products. Who could blame them? Tech was booming, and winning companies seemed to fuel their success with a steady diet of new talent, who were attracted by the promise of "cool" work environments, work-hard/play-hard cultures, and the potential to strike it rich with stock options. But it didn't work at Xerox. Even though the company succeeded in attracting new talent to the organization, the unintended consequence of all the effort was not only an increase in compensation expense, but also an increase in turnover among its most experienced engineers, who left the organization because they felt that they didn't fit in anymore. And because Xerox was a company that made substantial profits by developing new applications for its existing technology, the loss of those engineers had a direct impact on profit margins. To make matters worse, the new engineering talent that had come to Xerox to be innovators turned over as well, once they realized the company's desire to be a fast-moving high-technology innovator was inconsistent with the importance of incremental process improvement and evolutionary engineering.

The point is, talent is important, and not for its own sake, but because it makes business sense. Talent is a source of competitive advantage, and having the right talent aligned with strategy and organization delivers results. As we have described, strategy, organization, and leadership are the core ingredients of the recipe for lasting business success, but it is the talent that prepares the meal.

But having great talent isn't enough. The New York Yankees perennially have the highest payroll in Major League Baseball and "buy" the seemingly best players available, but they don't win the World Series every year. As Michael Lewis explored so well in his best-selling book *Moneyball*, a team with a much, much lower payroll can compete head to head with much deeper-pocketed teams by using fresh approaches to talent analysis.[3] For example, athletes who excel in high school and college don't necessarily mature into successful major leaguers. A traditional approach to talent acquisition— in professional baseball, at least—is to simply look for a "phenom" with a high batting average and then bid for him. Lewis shows how the small-overhead Oakland Athletics were able to use an entirely different set of metrics for its talent searches. On-base percentages were discovered to be a far more desirable trait in major league prospects, Lewis explains. In order to create Shockproof businesses, leaders must be diligent in how they manage talent, and execute a Shockproof approach, composed of the following four critical elements:

*Talent Acquisition*: Effective sourcing, assessment, and selection are essential factors in executing against talent acquisition objectives. These processes can range from highly complex and formal methods that rely on job boards and other Internet technology, psychological assessments, and predictive indicators to more informal approaches whereby businesses use professional networks, references, and informal assessments of cultural fit.

The right approach for talent acquisition is specific to your business and very much a function of the talent you seek. Unfortunately, many organizations gloss over this point and treat talent acquisition as nothing more than filling open job requisitions as fast as they can. This approach often results in mismatched talent and missed opportunities to bring in people who can take the business to the next level.

Excellence in talent acquisition begins with determining what types of roles, skills, and people are required for success. Because talent is such a valuable and important asset, and because the cost of bad decisions is so high, smart businesses conduct "make, buy, or rent" analyses to determine their talent requirements before beginning the recruitment process. They begin sourcing and evaluating candidates only after they have gained a clear sense of the skills, competencies, values, and experience that will be most valuable. In some cases, the best candidates may have a great deal in common with current staff. In others, it's just the opposite. In all cases, they don't stop the acquisition process after induction day; rather, they continue to support new recruits until they're fully *in* the organization and up to speed in their new roles.

*Talent Deployment*: Placing the right people in the right jobs is a hallmark of Shockproof organizations. These businesses maintain a thorough understanding of the talent they have and the talent they need. They have a clear sense of the relative value of key positions, and make sure that they assign their best talent to the jobs that have the greatest impact. By segmenting their talent the way most businesses segment their customers, these organizations are smart about how they allocate resources. Furthermore, realizing that talent is always in flux, they continuously assess the alignment between their talent needs and the talent they have on board. Leaders in talent deployment maintain detailed talent inventories and compare their company's talent needs to both current and anticipated bench strength.

Like a chess master, organizations that excel in talent deployment think several moves ahead. They realize the time it takes to develop a great plant manager, biostatistician, or product designer, and are deliberate in staffing "feeder" roles to build bench strength to meet their expected talent needs. This practice is evident in organizations that hire employees into rotational assignment programs, with the objective of teaching new recruits the business prior to assigning them to permanent positions.

*Talent Development:* Talent development represents a tremendous opportunity for businesses to protect and increase the value of the talent they already have. Often thought of as the work of the Human Resources or training departments, talent development is an area where leaders and employees can work together to make their organizations more Shockproof.

When leaders and employees share accountability for developing talent, the result is much like what happens when you hire a personal trainer or a tennis coach to improve performance. Practice becomes more focused and deliberate, and both student and coach have the same goal. The coach can't exercise or play on behalf of his or her student, and the student must take personal accountability in order to improve his or her performance. Similarly, employees in Shockproof organizations are clear about their objectives, know their strengths, and seek out opportunities to learn and grow. They avail themselves of on-the-job learning opportunities, seek out informal mentors, and make the most of performance management and development processes designed to help them develop new skills and abilities.

As business conditions change, talent can quickly become obsolete. Only by keeping up with or, better yet, anticipating new developments can businesses and their people maintain a competitive edge. Organizations that share a Shockproof mentality think of talent development as they chart new directions and strategies. They create formal and informal learning opportunities, matched to their business priorities and their employees' capabilities and needs. Employees in Shockproof organizations see the value in continuous development, and engage with leaders and colleagues to help identify and close their own performance gaps, so that they can contribute at higher levels.

*Rewarding Talent:* Rewards often serve as the lens through which employees view their relationships with their employers or prospective employers. Whereas many people think of rewards as a paycheck, Shockproof organizations take a more integrated view and include not only compensation but also benefits, culture, career, and work environment. These offerings form the basis for what is sometimes termed an *exchange relationship*, in which the employer offers rewards to its employees in exchange for their contributions to the employer's success. This view, which has been persistent and evolving over the past quarter century, lays a foundation for an emerging Shockproof approach to rewards.

As the "war for talent" has begun to take a different route, employers and employees are finding themselves increasingly on the same side. They realize that to succeed they must work together to find better, more sustainable solutions. In these cases, the expectation of zero-sum bargaining between adversaries is diminishing, and both parties—employers and employees—are beginning to think about rewards from a new perspective. Leaders in these organizations apply the Interpersonal Lens to understand the needs and values of the people with whom they work. They apply the Systems Lens to develop integrated rewards that facilitate lasting, mutually beneficial relationships between employers, employees, and the changing context in which they interact. Rewards in these organizations are hardwired into core business and operational processes and facilitate the alignment between strategy, organization, talent, and leadership. They are purpose-built, delivering value to their recipients, who recognize and expect that rewards will evolve as business conditions change.

In order for talent to credibly take its place as the most valuable asset for organizations, employers and employees must first recognize and then seize the opportunity to win, by having the right people in the right jobs doing the right things. To do so, leaders and staff must demonstrate excellence in acquiring, deploying, developing, and rewarding their current and future talent—all while maintaining alignment between talent, strategy, organization, and leadership (see Figure 5.1).

Tough duty, right? Well, yes and no. In the pages that follow, you'll read examples of organizations and leaders that excel in these areas every day and whose results are impressive. Their Shockproof approaches to managing talent are in many ways common sense. What is uncommon are the results they achieve. And what makes the difference

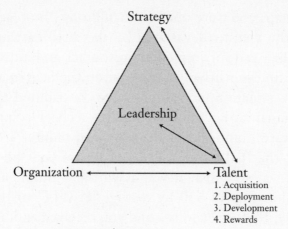

Figure 5.1 The Shockproof Model

is that Shockproof organizations actually apply their common sense to hardwire talent into how they do business.

## TALENT ACQUISITION: THE PEOPLE WHO GOT YOU HERE WON'T GET YOU THERE

The offer of a cool new phone, unlimited minutes, and a low monthly rate is just too good to pass up. Besides, having three important calls drop last week while you were driving through dead zones has strengthened your resolve to change mobile phone providers. You had held off doing this for years because you didn't want to change your phone number but had finally decided to make a move when you learned about something called "number portability." You still don't understand how it works or why, but knowing that your phone number is yours to keep is all that matters. You've learned that in your fast-paced life your mobile phone has become much more than a device to call Mom.

Perhaps you were one of the millions who reached out to help the victims devastated by the 2010 earthquake in Haiti. The need for immediate resources and aid was crucial, and time-sensitive. In the past, in the face of a similar disastrous situation, you might have contributed to a charity or humanitarian effort by mailing a check or providing a credit card number over the phone or online. This time, however, the Red Cross asked you to use your phone in a different way to assist. It was a swift and simple action to make a donation of $10 by texting "HAITI" to the number 90999. It took seconds—and you received an immediate confirmation that $10 for Haitian earthquake relief would be added to your next phone bill. The number 90999 is what is known as a *common short code*, a personal, timely, and interactive method of instantly communicating to a vast audience, and by using this technology you became a part of an effort that raised more than $30 million in record time to help the citizens of Haiti. You've never really thought about how this technology works, and as you stop and think about it, you wonder if it's possible to elect a president with a text message vote?

Sometime in the next year or so, you will probably buy or rent a full-length feature film online. The content will be delivered electronically and you will be able to watch it at home on your TV, at the coffee shop on your laptop, and even on your mobile phone as you commute to work by bus or train. You won't be able to make a copy of it, but the content you paid for will be available to you whenever, wherever, and however you want it. You'll be able to do this because a group of companies in the entertainment, software, hardware, retail, infrastructure, and delivery industries have decided to create a "Digital Rights Locker" to keep track of the content they have access to and the devices they have registered to access their content.

All of this is possible because of a company that many people have never heard of—Neustar, Inc. Neustar was founded in 1996 to meet the demands that arose when the U.S. government mandated local number portability. Today, the company delivers addressing, interoperability, and infra-structure services worldwide, to communication service providers, enterprises, associations, governments, and regulatory agencies. As it says on Neustar's web site, "Decades ago, communication was simple. Every telephone call had a fixed starting point and end point. However, with the advent of local number portability, the Internet and mobility, the routing of communications among thousands of service providers worldwide has become infinitely more complex."[4] And, as a result, so have the challenges Neustar faces every day.

Neustar's story is remarkable and one that provides a pertinent example of the role talent acquisition can play in Shockproofing an organization. In 1996, Neustar's prede-cessor organization (the Communications Industry Services operating unit of Lockheed Martin) won its original contract to provide number portability services. Three years later, it was spun off from Lockheed as a private company, and in 2005 Neustar became a public company. Guided by expe-rienced telecommunications industry leaders, the company grew quickly through this period, adding services such as common short codes and expanding its footprint in the wire-less telecommunications industry. At the same time, Neustar began entering the Internet Protocol (IP) arena, acquiring and managing new domain names like .biz, .net, and both .cn (for China) and .tw (for Taiwan), to complement its core number portability contract. (Internet Protocol is the method, or protocol, used to transmit data from one computer to another on the Internet. Each computer on the Internet has a unique identifier, called an IP address, that makes communication over the network possible.)

As the company began evolving its strategy, several members of the senior leadership team, who had helped bring the company through its IPO, moved on. This presented both a major challenge and, as it turns out, a great opportunity. Many businesses faced with a similar situation would have replaced the departed executives with new leaders cut from the same telecom cloth. After all, the company had been very successful as a result of its core telecommunications services, so why fix what wasn't broken? But Neustar took a different path. It seized the opportunity to acquire new—and in many ways different—leaders to chart the company's second act and continue its history of high growth.

The future, Neustar decided, was in IP. Building on its core expertise in managing and maintaining neutral networks and databases, Neustar saw the opportunity to, in the words of Doug Arnold, Senior Vice President of Human Resources, "retool and reimagine the company . . . to continue its high growth and become a global, IP business."[5] While this vision presented an exciting future, it was not one Neustar was ready for at the time. In rethinking the business, Arnold and newly hired President and COO Lisa Hook (named CEO in October 2010) recognized that the company needed leaders with different skill sets than those that had made Neustar successful in its early years. To enter new, more competitive markets around the globe, the company would need leaders with experience developing and marketing new products and a track record of growing businesses quickly. Because of its history as an industry-level infrastructure service provider, these were not areas where Neustar was strong, as evidenced by Arnold's comment that when he "joined the company, only one person in the company had the word 'marketing' in his title."

In a sense, Neustar had arrived at the realization that the "people who got us here, won't get us there." With the business changing, and faced with several gaps in its leadership team lineup, Neustar was very much at risk for a substantial shock. Faced with the proverbial challenge of changing the tires on a moving car, the company had two choices: staff for today or staff for tomorrow. While the answer seems obvious, most businesses in a similar situation succumb to the temptation of putting the urgent before the important and go about "plugging holes." Our experience is that taking this approach is like applying a Band-Aid when you need stitches. Neustar made the more difficult decision. It hunkered down and determined where the company needed to go, then set about acquiring the talent that would help them get there. The discipline it takes to be clear about talent acquisition needs, and the fortitude required to do what it takes to find the right people (even if it takes a little longer), is the essence of effective talent acquisition. It would have been easier to move existing employees "up the organization chart" to fill executive roles, or go back to the same fishing holes to quickly recruit new leaders, but Neustar stuck to its plan.

Fueled by a sense of urgency, Neustar sharpened its executive recruiting focus on commercial skill sets and high-tech experience. Over the course of two years, the company changed the composition of its leadership team by filling 45 percent of its positions at the Vice President level and above with new hires. Arnold says that it "all began with strategy . . . determining where the business needs to go, what sort of people we need to have, and what sort of culture; . . . and we have accelerated our development by finding the *right* people."

As Neustar embarked on its effort to recruit new leaders and acquire new skills, Arnold noticed an interesting trend in the new executives he hired. "While more intuitive than conscious at first, we made offers to people who talked about the accomplishments of teams during their interviews. As these people came on board, the culture began to evolve. We began to see that we were creating a more collaborative culture, liked what we saw, and as a result started seeking this attribute in our recruits." Months later, it's "remarkable what cohesiveness we have," says Arnold, "considering how new so many people are to the organization. People are rooting for each other, trading leads, and always looking for ways to help out."

What Doug Arnold describes is an example of two of the five Cs of Shockproofing in action—*cultivate* and *collaborate*. (The five Cs of Alignment are described in detail in Chapter 6). By recruiting new leaders who value collaboration, Neustar effectively changed its culture more so than it could have through months of offsite retreats, commemorative water bottles, and corporate email blasts. The executives they hired came on board and acted differently than the people they replaced. They understood that their interests were aligned, and engaged their organizations in working together to achieve the company's highest priorities.

When asked about Neustar's thinking about building versus buying talent, Arnold notes that, "The marketplace is changing so quickly that going out and buying a whole new capability is probably a better idea than trying to develop it yourself." The business imperative is clear: "We've got to get there first and get there fast." Adding to this challenge is that Neustar is not a brand-new business; it has long-standing customers and a tenured workforce. Arnold knows the difficulties of "building a cohesive and desirable culture when you are bringing in so many new people and already have an existing culture." In response, senior leaders are spending more time out in the workforce and less time in their offices. Neustar is "parading out examples" of new behaviors and values, such as collaboration and innovation. Every six weeks, the company holds a "NeuView" meeting that is viewable from anywhere in the world. Senior leaders participate, but the stars of the show are usually younger employees who present their experiences developing and implementing new ideas. Says Arnold, "The employee population is inspired; they like what they see—that we are being aggressive in the marketplace, that we are getting into new businesses, and that our management practices are improving to prepare us for new growth."

Thus Neustar, a technology company that like so many could have stagnated as a result of its early success, Shock-proofed itself through talent acquisition. Turning what could have been a leadership crisis into an opportunity, the company developed a clear vision of the talent it would need in the future, rather than trying to replicate the talent that had made it successful in the past. By recruiting a group of leaders who valued collaboration and innovation, and who had experience growing competitive businesses, Neustar laid the foundation for continued success. Doug Arnold says that, "For me, the headline is that we have done it consciously. We've linked talent, strategy, and culture. We're building the strength to grow at the pace we need in the industries where we want to be successful."

## TALENT DEPLOYMENT: RIGHT PEOPLE, RIGHT PLACE, RIGHT TIME

Because acquiring great talent is so important, many businesses we know have placed big bets on staffing. They have purchased specialized software to track and manage applications, invested in social networking, and offered referral and sign-ing bonuses to improve their ability to attract the people they seek. And many do improve their ability to get "butts in seats" quickly and efficiently, but it's the organizations that consistently figure out where to put their talent that enjoy lasting success. These organizations realize that talent flow is dynamic, and regularly fine-tune and refine their efforts to make sure that their people are in the jobs where they can create the most value.

Like airlines that realize the importance of a frequent business traveler, or the bartender who knows his best custo-mers, these businesses recognize that managing jobs and peo-ple based on the value they deliver is good business. There's a reason the million-mile flyers stand in shorter lines and get on the plane first: It's because they fly every week and pay full fare. And that guy who's getting a round on the house? He's at the bar every Friday night after softball, brings his friends and tips well. To the untrained eye, treating customers dif-ferently may seem unfair. But looking closer it becomes clear that doing so couldn't be more fair. These are examples of customer *segmentation*, a go-to-market approach rooted in the use of the Value lens. Leaders and employees who apply this lens understand how value is both created and destroyed in their businesses, and act accordingly. They design prod-ucts and pricing to attract and retain their most valuable cus-tomers, and invest less in those who are less profitable.

Smart businesses are beginning to apply these same prin-ciples to the management of talent. To varying degrees they are analyzing the drivers of value in their organizations and creating roles and deploying talent with the clear objective of maximizing that value. In thinking though these decisions, leaders use the Value Lens to manage talent. They make it a priority to answer questions such as:

- Are we allocating enough of the right resources to doing the things that matter most? Or are we overinvesting in less critical areas of our business?

- Which roles are most critical to our success?

- What does the talent inventory look like today? How effectively is talent deployed? (Are the right people in the right jobs?)

- What is the nature and size of the gap between current and future talent needs?

A case in point is the Martin Agency of Richmond, Virginia. This award-winning advertising agency (*AdWeek*'s 2010 U.S. Agency of the Year, among other accolades) is responsible for such iconic creations as the GEICO Gecko, Cavemen, the UPS whiteboard campaign, as well as Walmart's "Save money. Live better." ads, and many others that have become woven into the fabric of American popular culture. Ad pros know their stuff is working when their clients rate inclusion in the late-night monologues of David Letterman, Jay Leno, and Jimmy Fallon. And while the agency's fame is very much a function of its client work, its success over time speaks in many ways to how the firm manages talent.

Founded in 1965, Martin is no fly-by-night start-up. Its high standards, disciplined approach, and attention to aligning people and work set it apart and have made its growth possible. According to Chairman and Chief Executive Officer John Adams, "The key difference between agencies that grow and those that don't is the ability to grow beyond the span of control of the key people. In some cases, agencies go out of business because one of the key people leaves."[6] This risk is exacerbated by growth, and the typical response to growth in the advertising agency has been to add layers. Adds Mike Hughes, Martin's President and Creative Director, "We looked at how other agencies were structuring as they got bigger . . . and typically the copy writers [in a big agency] could be seven people removed from the Creative Director. I didn't want to go to that structure."[7] Hughes worried that, "In the words of the legendary advertising icon, Jay Chiat, 'We're in an industry where people begin to wonder how big are we going to get before we get bad?'" So instead of following the traditional route, Martin did something unusual: It named 14 Creative Directors, contrary to the conventional wisdom of naming one or two in order to concentrate control and maintain consistent standards. "We took people that we thought would be best at it—some were pretty young writers and art directors—and made it their job to head up several accounts and manage and mentor people who might well be working on other accounts." According to CEO Adams, Martin made this change because, "We felt the need to distribute decision-making accountability closer to the ground level and to make sure that those people could make significant decisions on the battlefield." He added, "I was nervous, because I was so comfortable with everything going through Mike [Hughes] . . . but people stepped up."

Martin extends this approach even further because its Creative Directors are not only directly connected to Mike Hughes, they are directly connected to their clients. "One thing that is unmistakable," says Hughes, "is that the best creative work is a combination of what is true about the client and what is true about the person who is doing the work. What I want is for our people to put themselves 'in the work.' You can see it so visibly in some of our best-known work. Literally, for UPS, Creative Director Andy Azula was the guy *in* the commercials drawing on the whiteboard. For a lot of our Walmart work, the songs were written by a guy here, from his heart. People ask me sometimes why the [GEICO] Gecko has so many different personalities, and that's because when we put different writers on the Gecko, they can put their personality in him. The client has never stopped us from doing this, and they have felt the benefit of having our writers so deeply invested. At some places, they go through crazy things . . . they think about, 'What can Pop-N-Fresh do? What's true for Pop-N-Fresh?' What we have to do is what's true to GEICO and what's true to the creators of the work . . . and it comes through that way."

Talent segmentation and deployment is an area where art meets science. Sometimes, as in the case of the Martin Agency, value, fit, and alignment are visible to those who know the talent personally, know what to look for, and are in a position to make the right decisions. Other times, speed and scale require a more systematic approach. This is the case in the world of large-scale government contracting, a business where misalignment between people and skill requirements can put multimillion-dollar contracts at risk and where vacant positions result in lost revenue and profit erosion. Also, because most employees in this industry are funded by the specific contracts to which they are assigned, it is common for their employment to be terminated when their contracts end. As a result, many government contractors let people go one day because a contract ends and the next day begin looking for identical replacements to fill the requirements of a newly signed deal. By most estimates, the average cost to fill a position in this industry is around $5,000; and hundreds, if not thousands, of positions come open when a contract is awarded. What this means is that keeping contracts staffed is mission-critical, and that the people responsible for doing so are perpetually on the hot seat.

Larry Clifton is no stranger to pressure, and he definitely knows what it's like to be responsible for a mission-critical operation. Clifton was the Aerial Port Commanding Officer for Air Force One during the Clinton Administration, and his team had the rare distinction of being the only one in history to achieve a 100 percent reliability rate (the Air Force equivalent of on-time departure rate). Clifton's latest mission is to lead the talent acquisition and deployment efforts of CACI International Inc., a $3 billion government contractor that provides professional and IT services to support defense and civilian agencies. As Senior Vice President of Recruiting and Workforce Management for a company that employs more than 13,000 employees around the world, Clifton continues to live mission-critical issues every day. "What I've learned, whether it's Air Force One, working in the Pentagon, or in corporate roles, is that it really is all about the people. Everyone talks about it, but you've got to hire the right people to be successful."[8]

Charged with creating a centralized recruiting function for CACI, Clifton saw the opportunity to contribute significantly to the bottom line. "In our business, it's common to let people go when they come 'off contract,'" he said. "I looked around and thought that we were spending too much money on recruiting." He saw opportunities to increase revenue and profitability by reducing the number of positions filled externally and cutting the time to hire. Doing these key things would reduce the number of vacant revenue-producing positions and contribute directly to the bottom line. "At the senior leadership level," Clifton explained, "very few companies in our industry know exactly what contract every employee is on, or what their skill set, or education level, or security clearance is." But under Larry Clifton's leadership, CACI built a database that put this information at his fingertips. "If I see a contract will end in six months, I can start working to try to place people ahead of the game. This increased our 'saves' [reassignments of employees who would have been terminated at the end of a contract] by 49 percent, to 701, in 2009." This is an excellent example of applying the Value Lens to make CACI more Shockproof. Clifton realizes that vacant positions on sold contracts destroy value, so the Recruiting and Workforce Management team's focus on "saving" talent is perfectly aligned with the company's business priorities. This approach also demonstrates how using the Systems Lens helps leaders recognize powerful opportunities to drive results, by thinking through the possible interrelationships between business units, functions, processes, and people. Whereas many competitors' recruiting organizations focus narrowly on filling openings, and don't worry about talent retention, CACI's group captures value by quickly redeploying the talent it has already invested in bringing on board.

Furthermore, though Clifton's initial objective was to use the database to capture money that was being left on the table in this way, he is evolving his approach to include predictive modeling, as well. His intent is to "take it to the next level by tying the model to the strategic plan, the financials, and the business development pipeline." This enables CACI to maintain continuous alignment between talent acquisition and deployment efforts and the company's most critical priorities. As the strategy evolves and priorities change, Clifton's approach is to adjust the flow and assignment of people accordingly. He and his colleagues can tell which opportunities are coming due and begin to "handicap" the probability of winning, along with the implications for where talent will be needed. Based on this, CACI knows what jobs it needs to fill and can, according to Clifton, "figure out which jobs we'll fill internally and externally, and where we see gaps between the talent we have and the talent we need so we can figure out if it makes sense to train a current employee or hire a new one."

Furthering CACI's efforts to better deploy talent, the Recruiting and Workforce Management team has built an internal job board so employees who are interested in changing jobs can do so without leaving the company. This is a common practice in many commercial businesses but "is unheard of in government contracting," said Clifton, and represents "a significant change management challenge for our managers" because of the operational and financial consequences of having to fill vacancies resulting from employee transfers. CACI has established rules and processes to ensure that the voluntary redeployment of talent does not disrupt its work for clients, and Clifton reasons that doing so is worthwhile because he would rather have good "employees leave their jobs than leave the company."

During Larry Clifton's tenure, CACI has reduced its cost per hire from $7,100 to $3,400. Considering that the company hired more than 3,500 employees last year, that's a savings of nearly $13 million, in addition to over $2 million savings attributable to the 701 employees who were redeployed instead of terminated—not to mention the added revenue generated by reducing the time required to fill the new positions.

Global pharmaceutical leader Novartis also uses the deployment of talent as a strategic advantage. Because of the company's breadth of expertise and sheer scale (over $44 billion in 2009 sales and 100,000 employees worldwide), Novartis deploys talent deliberately to build great leaders throughout its business.

At Novartis, the drive to produce extraordinary general managers is unrelenting; it begins with recruiting only those with high business acumen and people leadership skills and potential. Employees who demonstrate high potential are identified to rise fast in the organization through a broad set of experiences that stretch them outside of the comfort of their background and truly test their ceiling of capability. Performance matters in every assignment, and executives and HR business partners invest weeks every year pouring over the accomplishments and struggles of top talent to determine whether they are on track for new challenges or have hit the limit of their abilities. As Frank Maness, Vice President of Human Resources of Novartis Corporation, the U.S. holding company, points out, "There is risk in stretching key talent this way, but here it is mitigated by a willingness to confront underperformance quickly, and an abiding knowledge that the focus and investment across the organization is creating a deeper bench."[9]

While it may not be for everyone, those who progress through developmental assignments have the opportunity to learn how to absorb shocks firsthand. As a result, this ability is resident within each manager and executive as they advance. They have already been challenged beyond their comfort zones, and the organization has had a "trial run," in many cases, of how a leader will respond to shocks to the organization.

## TALENT DEVELOPMENT

> I have never let my schooling interfere
> with my education.
> —Mark Twain

Talent and what it must do to succeed is continuously evolving. Changes in the economy, industry developments, regional trends, cultural evolution, and new priorities within individual businesses themselves will render even the highest-level performer obsolete if he or she doesn't regularly hone the skills necessary to perform his or her job. Like typewriters, eight-track tape players, and rotary-dial telephones, many of the things we once held dear are quick to lose their relevance.

Employers and employees often look to talent development as the means for renewing and recalibrating their capabilities. Those who do it well make use of formal and informal learning opportunities and share accountability for results among key stakeholders. When employees take ownership of their careers and their development, and the companies they work for provide clarity regarding expectations and resources, the result is more meaningful, more relevant development. Organizations where this happens are better able to resist shocks because they maintain alignment between their business imperatives and the learning and preparation necessary to achieve results. Susan Peters, GE's Chief Learning Officer, was quoted in *BusinessWeek* as saying that the company is "working on '21st century' attributes." The same article relates that John Lynch, Senior Vice President for Corporate Human Resources, believes that "the beauty of GE's system is that it can be adapted rapidly to a shifting environment. Under Welch, for example, the prized skills were cost-cutting, efficiency, and deal making. Then Immelt came in, calling for risk-taking, customer focus, and innovation."[10]

As we've indicated, *development* isn't just another word for training; it includes the competencies that distinguish exemplary performance, formal and informal learning experiences, individual development planning, and career paths, as well as the performance management processes that facilitate these efforts. In contrast to old-fashioned development programs where learning was expected to take place only in the classroom, organizations that now successfully blend these efforts often follow the 70/20/10 rule, whereby 70 percent of development takes place through on-the-job-learning and problem solving, 20 percent through formal and informal mentorship, and 10 percent through formal training. This approach is not only more consistent with how adults learn (by doing); it is more productive, as it harnesses intellect and energy to solve real problems in real time.

Founded in 1875, the American Bankers Association (ABA) is the principal trade association representing the banking industry. The ABA represents banks of all sizes and charters, but the majority of its members are banks with less than $165 million in assets. With the vision of being "recognized as the most effective financial services trade association, to which all banks choose to belong, and to be one of the best places to work in Washington, DC," the ABA's staff of fewer than 400 has faced the formidable task of representing its members' interests and addressing their educational needs in the face of historic industry events.

Despite the banking industry's challenges, and the corresponding decrease in dues and attendance-based revenue at its conferences and seminars, the ABA has redoubled its commitment to developing talent. According to Bob Eady, Executive Vice President and Chief Financial Officer, the focus followed ABA's 2007 merger with America's Community Bankers (ACB) and "soul searching at the executive level regarding the importance of people to the organization."[11] This perspective has become stronger with the realization that 20 percent or more of the organization will be eligible to retire within the next five years. Adds Howard Walseman, Senior Vice President of Human Resources, "One of the things we have made the decision *not* to cut is the expense related to professional development. He noted that at other organizations the "knee jerk reaction [to financial pressure] is to cut training and development, [but] that has not happened here."[12]

To prepare its next cadre of leaders to meet the challenges of the future, the ABA created a comprehensive approach to development, dubbed "LeadershipABA." Created by a cross-functional team of experienced ABA executives, LeadershipABA's stated goal "is to build future generations of leaders and expand their learning opportunities beyond their individual jobs." The thinking behind the ABA's approach exemplifies the application of a Shockproof approach to development.

Essentially, LeadershipABA is a partnership between employees and their employer. As Eady put it, "In the past we had tuition assistance programs and generic management training, but this is different—it's based on shared responsibility. Participants realize that we really have added a whole other set of challenges on top of their 'regular jobs.'" When asked to describe the program, Walseman said that it is "a blend of the ways that participants can improve their understanding of the organization while addressing critical needs, so it is anchored in the ABA's highest priorities. The corporate goals themselves are reflective of the organization's needs and, ultimately, the needs of members." Because participants are accountable for addressing big issues, LeadershipABA is a "departure from the past where executive vice presidents would sit around a table, identify the 15 to 20 most critical issues, and take responsibility for addressing them themselves," added Walseman.

Perhaps the most visible component of the ABA's approach to developing talent is the creation of interdepartmental teams that involve nearly 25 percent of the workforce.

Led by a dozen of the ABA's high-potential future leaders, these teams are charged with achieving an objective that is directly linked to one of ABA's annual corporate goals. One project is to build ABA's membership among banks with $1 billion to $10 billion or more in assets. "This is an area where we haven't been as strong, so this team is focused on banks of this size that are not currently ABA members," remarked Eady. Leaders are assigned to projects outside of their core areas of technical expertise, to drive innovation and build resourcefulness. Thus, as Eady explained, "The person leading the project is not in the Membership department where most of the membership efforts are focused." This is done to support LeadershipABA's objectives to expand participants' understanding of enterprise issues, address complex business issues that span groups, collaborate effectively, and improve team leadership and relationship skills.

"Getting participants to self-direct their development" is an important objective, as well, says Walseman. "They take several assessments and create their own individual development plans where they identify some skills they need to improve or knowledge they need to build. This is something they agree to with their assigned mentors, and participants are accountable for making progress in these areas."

Another element of the development effort is group discussion sessions where participants read cases and talk about key leadership concepts relevant to the ABA, such as strategic thinking, leading and managing teams, corporate culture, and core values. These events are supplemented with "Business Leader Dialogues" with prominent leaders from outside the ABA, who meet with participants to discuss their experiences and lessons they've learned in their careers. Speakers have represented a diversity of leadership styles, and ranged from Elizabeth A. Duke, Governor of the

Federal Reserve Board, to *Fast Company* magazine Founding Editor William Taylor, and Karl A. Racine, Venable LLP's Managing Partner (voted one of the 50 Most Influential Minority Lawyers in America).[13]

The strength of this approach lies in its comprehensiveness and relative simplicity. Sure, it's hard work and puts additional demands on top of the participants' already busy schedules, but the projects are "real world" and aligned with the ABA's highest priorities. As Howard Walseman said, "There is a deliberate effort to make the curriculum flexible, as well as in setting corporate goals to address issues that are important to the ABA and its members."

The ABA's approach is an ideal model for how to hardwire talent development to strategy. And because interdepartmental team projects are expected to change to correspond with the ABA's annual corporate goals, they ensure that talent development remains in alignment with the organization's objectives. Walseman and the LeadershipABA development team are working to Shockproof a trade association whose members are experiencing the greatest shock since the stock market crashed in 1929. Inherent in the program's design and execution is a regular and continuous *calibration* (another of the five Cs) between strategy and talent, intended to ensure that the ABA and its leaders are well positioned to help their members respond to changes in the economic, regulatory, and political environments.

Hudson Australia/New Zealand has had notable success hardwiring business imperatives through its leadership development programs, as well. A division of $700 million professional staffing and talent management firm Hudson Highland Group, Inc., this company named Mark Steyn President and CEO in 2008. Steyn had little experience in the recruiting and talent management business so as a first step, he set about getting to know the business he had been charged to lead. According to Tracy Noon, Hudson Australia/New Zealand's Chief Human Resources Officer, Steyn returned from his travels and described what he initially encountered as "permafrost" in his leadership layers—the further he went down the organization, the less alignment, understanding, and support for the business strategy. Steyn believed that to be successful, his leaders needed to be effective in "translating strategy into action at the ground level," and that "no matter how enthusiastic senior and middle managers were about the strategy, they would not be able to do so"[14] unless they built new capabilities.

Faced with this challenge, Noon and Steyn applied a progressive approach to building leaders' capabilities. Rather than just "teaching" them, they decided to engage the organization's top leaders in instituting a development program that they themselves would roll out to the organizations they led. "It was a really good example of experiential and action learning," said Noon. "The benefits were that these leaders had their own learning experience in developing the content, because it challenged them to refine their ideas and decide what was really important." As the Hudson team developed the program's content, Noon says they "realized that [they] had to drive it deeper into the organization, to frontline supervisors," in order to "get everyone speaking the same language and get the business in synch."

The team developed this program using "real [Hudson] data," explained Noon, rather than case examples, making the learning more relevant both to the program designers, as well as to the intended participants. And, they worked diligently to refine their strategy and business model along the way. Building the curriculum—based on Hudson's "SmartBusiness" program, designed by the company's European leadership team—created an opportunity for leaders to come together and advance not only their understanding of the business, but their perspective on the future, too. Unlike many leadership development programs that are designed by Human Resources, the SmartBusiness curriculum was created by the leaders themselves—all the way to the top. "What was really different about this was the engagement of the CEO and his team in developing and designing the content," remarked Noon. The result, she says, was "all levels of leadership singing from the same hymn sheet and using the same language and capabilities," effectively melting the "permafrost" Steyn had initially encountered. Steyn's "willingness to invest his own discretionary time and effort to be personally involved" in creating content stood out to Noon, and she believes that the leadership team's experience working together to create SmartBusiness helped them "get the various strands of strategy, structure, and people into alignment . . . , which helped them see how things hang together in ways that are not always evident at the 'helicopter level.'"

What about the program participants for whom Smart-Business was created? They were the ultimate beneficiaries of Hudson's efforts to link strategy development and strategy execution. In addition to working in an increasingly well-aligned business, Noon reports that participants "said it was the most relevant, most useful 'training program' they'd ever participated in. All of the feedback was extremely positive," and Hudson is continuing to refine its program to keep it fresh and relevant to its Australia/New Zealand business.

## SHOCKPROOF REWARDS
## TRY THE VEAL—OR, HOW CAN THE
## FOOD BE SO GOOD AND THE SERVICE SO BAD?

You've finally scored a table at the hottest new restaurant in town, complete with a celebrity chef and runway-model staff. The maître d' greets you and your date and lets you know that your table isn't ready yet but that it will only be a 15- or 20-minute wait. No worries. You're just happy to be there. All the foodies are buzzing about this place, and so far none of your friends have been able to get a reservation.

Finally, a very fashionably dressed host walks you and your date to a table, seats you, and with the panache of a matador, snaps open starched napkins and hands them to you. (This place has a maître d' *and* a host!). Your date is *very* impressed—this is one chic joint. After taking in the sights and sounds of all the beautiful people, you and your date decide it might be nice to order a bottle of wine. You wait for someone to appear to take your order. You wait some more. And wait. And wait. You try to catch someone's eye, but the only eyes looking your way are boring a hole into you, and they belong to your date. Soon you feel like you're back in second grade, raising your hand to get the teacher's attention, while server after server parades by, deftly avoiding making eye contact with you. You're feeling invisible. Then, from experience, it gradually dawns on you that the staff at this restaurant probably don't pool their tips; every server is looking out for him- or herself. A busboy finally comes over and says he's sorry he can't take your order but he will be happy to get your server. While you stew, it becomes obvious that the busboy isn't authorized to do anything other than fill water glasses, clear plates, and run messages.

*Finally*, your server arrives. She's very pleasant, but charmingly insistent that you order the Chef's Special Prix Fixe Menu that costs more than you paid for your first car. As she waxes eloquently about the French oysters, foie gras, and Nova Scotia lobster in a black truffle sauce, you are pretty sure she's thinking about how much she'll be getting paid tonight, rather than how much you'll enjoy your meal. And unbeknownst to you, in a parallel gastronomic universe, a behind-the-scenes black market is at work; there, chefs and bartenders trade steaks for cocktails, and the maître d' gets kickbacks from servers for seating big spenders in their section. As you make your selection from the à la carte side of the menu, you learn that the kitchen doesn't allow substitutions from the menu and that there's a charge for sharing dessert, and you begin to wonder if you're being punished for spurning your server's prix fixe recommendation.

Before your salad arrives, you decide that even if the food tonight is the best you've ever eaten, you'd rather dine on Kibbles 'n Bits than eat at this place ever again. More than likely, you'll just go back to your favorite neighborhood place, where the staff knows your name and how much you love steamed mussels in garlic and wine with a side of fries, and where the chef is happy to whip up something special for your nephew, the picky eater. At *your* joint, everyone you come into contact with seems happy to be there, including the patrons.

Walk into any restaurant and you'll see rewards at work. Every seasoned bartender has learned that when they give away a drink once, they get it back twice in tips. The old adage that "what gets rewarded gets done" is alive and well. This is why rewards are effective Shockproofing tools—because they drive behavior. They help employees understand what's important, what they need to do to be successful, and what's in it for them if they are successful. Designed and used appropriately, rewards contribute to results by strengthening alignment between talent and strategy. Left unattended, as they were in the fancy restaurant where you will never, ever, eat again, they can have devastating unintended consequences.

Our experience is that rewards can contribute significantly to Shockproofing organizations when they are:

- Managed as a core business process.
- Defined as more than just money.
- Simple in intent and design.
- Flexible and adaptable to change.

## The Case for Shockproof Rewards

With more than 33 million customers and 36,000-plus employees, T-Mobile is a good-sized fish in a giant pond. The company sets high standards for itself and is frequently recognized for its excellent results. In 2009, T-Mobile won the J.D. Power award for Highest Ranked Wireless Customer Service Performance[15] and was named one of *Fortune* magazine's 100 Best Companies to Work For—all in a year when the company froze salary increases (granted, it was to avoid the layoffs experienced by its industry competitors). The company aspires to be the "best place to perform" and exemplifies how rewards can be used creatively to protect itself from environmental shocks.

According to Bruce O'Neel, Senior Director of Employee Engagement and Rewards, "Rewards are a core element in how T-Mobile thinks about the rollout of new devices. We pick the best and the brightest to participate in our launches."[16]

Retail stores and customer care centers are assessed based
on their "fire in the belly," and those with the highest rat-
ings are selected to launch high-profile products. T-Mobile
encourages this friendly competition, and the winning teams
value the recognition they receive from the company and
from their coworkers. It's all part of the culture, says O'Neel:
"Teams hold video pep rallies for each other, and are genuinely excited by each other's success." In some ways, this is a
strategy of necessity for T-Mobile. As O'Neel puts it, "We
can't outspend AT&T and Verizon in marketing and advertising, so we have to win through people." It works. The
teams selected to introduce T-Mobile's HD2 smartphone
sold through their inventory in two weeks, versus a bench-
mark of 45 to 60 days.

On the surface, Serco Group plc and T-Mobile have
very little in common. T-Mobile has a strong consumer
brand in the United States and Serco, though it is one of
the world's leading service and outsourcing companies is
unknown to even those who are served directly by the company. Headquartered in the United Kingdom, this FTSE
100 company employs more than 70,000 employees in 30
countries. Serco's customers hire the company to manage 192,000 square miles of airspace in five countries, provide critical traffic management systems for nearly 11,000
miles of roadway, operate railways, protect borders, operate prisons, manage health care services, support the armed
forces, run major administration processes, and maintain
facilities. In North America, Serco's business has grown
rapidly since establishing its presence in 1988 and acquiring Resources Consultants Inc. (RCI) in 2007. According
to Louis Montgomery, Serco North America's Senior Vice
President of Human Resources, "Serco knew that the DOD
[Department of Defense] was a huge market and wanted to

get a footprint there, and RCI was a company that had a very deep presence in that area."[17]

The acquisition increased substantially the scale and complexity of Serco's North American operations. Montgomery joined the company in 2006 and soon realized the core role rewards played in achieving Serco's business objectives. It was clear that in the highly competitive North American labor market, Serco's "U.K.-style programs" were impeding the company's ability to "attract, develop, and retain the people we needed to grow as an organization, and to move up the value chain," he explained. The Serco North America team was successful in working with their colleagues in the United Kingdom to improve the design and competitiveness of their rewards programs; they found that the changes they made were essential in propelling the company's growth. They saw in rewards a core business process, one that was essential to their ability to compete successfully for talent and, as a result, for customers.

Then, in 2008, barely two years after Montgomery's arrival and the realignment of Serco's North American rewards programs, Serco North America doubled in size through the acquisition of SI International. With service lines complementary to those of Serco's existing business, SI gave the company greater scale and breadth. As Montgomery puts it, "In this market, size matters, and you need to be big enough to be a relevant player, because otherwise your customer may not view you as credible." Knowing their industry and their customers, Serco's leaders applied the Systems Lens to determine that the path forward would require a transformational acquisition.

Serco had determined the need to grow—and not just because it wanted to be a bigger player. Combining with SI

International represented an opportunity to acquire new capabilities that would enable the company to move up the value chain toward greater profitability. According to Montgomery, it was for this reason that Serco's leadership team decided "to integrate the organizations as quickly as possible, so that as of Day One we would operate as a unified team, and we would move as quickly as we could to make other changes to make us look and feel, and actually be, a combined organization." Looking through the Change Lens, Montgomery concluded that, "While it's relatively easy to acquire a company, it's way more difficult to integrate one into a seamless entity."

To achieve this objective, Serco once again turned to rewards, because as Montgomery puts it, "Rewards literally touch every employee." As the core instrument for "harmonizing the two legacy workforces," rewards became a driver of integration at Serco. And rather than following the common practice of replacing the acquired firm's policies and programs with those of the acquirer, Serco took the unusual step of "developing new programs that would be the best for the combined organization," explained Montgomery.

Reflecting on his nearly five years with Serco, Louis Montgomery said, "We set the strategy and then we put in place the rewards infrastructure that enabled us to attract and retain the kinds of talent that we needed to attract and retain. Had we not addressed these issues early on we would not have been able to successfully integrate SI International, nor would we have been able to bring on the people we needed to support our growth."

The best Shockproof rewards are those that comprise something more than a paycheck. Organizations where rewards equal money are the most prone to shock because they have only one tool in their toolbox, and competitors may emerge at any moment with a bigger hammer. As we have noted, the most effective Shockproof rewards are multidimensional, often integrating some combination of compensation, benefits, culture, and career with the evolving context in which every business exists. In this way, rewards serve as a lens (see Figure 5.2) as well, one through which employees and potential employees view their relationship with an employer.

**Figure 5.2 Shockproof Businesses Realize That Rewards Are More Than Just Pay**

## HOW TO THINK ABOUT REWARDS

While very much an example of how to apply the Systems and Value Lenses, the integrated approach to rewards also relies on the Interpersonal Lens, because in order to be valued by employees, rewards need to reflect an appreciation of what is important to them, not just to the employer.

T-Mobile recognizes the interconnected nature of effective rewards and has reorganized its Human Resources Center of Excellence functions along the lines of Employee Brand, Employee Talent Management, Employee Experience and Employee Engagement. These areas work in concert to develop and deliver a compelling employee value proposition, one that encompasses core rewards components such as base and variable pay, career progression, and rewards and recognition. Says Bruce O'Neel, "There are some great companies in the Seattle area, like Microsoft, Starbucks, Safeco Insurance, Nordstrom, and Amazon.com, and we are able to hold our own in the labor market—not because we try to be the highest payer but because the rewards we offer in combination are greater than the sum of their parts. Employees see this; they value it, and choose T-Mobile as the 'best place to perform.'"

Think of the greatest inventions of all time. No, not the microwave oven, the electric garage door opener, or the iPod; think of inventions from long ago that are still relevant today, like the wheel or the lever. These tools are valuable because they are simple, and because they work. They are basic, even minimalist, and for this reason they are highly adaptive to change. The same principle applies to rewards. The best solutions are the most simple, whether they involve compensation, benefits, culture, career, or even work environment.

We have certainly seen incentive compensation plans that would puzzle even the most advanced mathematicians. They have dozens of objectives and multiple levels, with different weightings and payout triggers—the sort of thing only a CPA could love. We've also seen health care benefits that are so complicated they actually make you sick during the enrollment process. Performance management and career development can be part of the problem, as well, when made up of lengthy and repetitive processes, reviews, and seven-layer approval requirements.

The principle of simplicity in Shockproof rewards program design stems from the Value Lens, in that it directs focus on what matters and disregards what does not. Marc Effron and Miriam Ort's excellent book *One Page Talent Management* is subtitled *Eliminating Complexity, Adding Value*, and makes exactly this point.[18] While working at Avon Products, the authors were asked to build and implement new talent management practices to support the turnaround of a $9 billion consumer products company. They write that, "What we delivered deviated from the more traditional views of how human resource (HR) and talent management practices should look and function. We had consciously worked to remove any extra features and complexity while simultaneously trying to add value into each to make the practices more effective." Effron and Ort believe that, "It is possible to increase talent depth and quality in the simplest, easiest way possible by creating the shortest path from the proven behavioral science to the desired business outcome." They go on to say, "Where organizations go wrong is that they fail to balance complexity with value as they build these processes. It is not that the additional components layered on—from highly detailed competency models to the extra hundred questions on an engagement survey—are technically wrong.

Many have sound behavioral science to support their inclusion. However, as each additional element is added, evaluating the trade-off between the complexity it brings to the *overall* process and the impact it will have on the original business objective is critical."

T-Mobile exemplifies this approach in the compensation and benefits components of its rewards program. In describing incentive compensation metrics, Bruce O'Neel said, "Before we had six measures that changed quarterly. Now we have two constant measures that everyone understands: growth and profit." Similarly, T-Mobile minimizes the moving parts in the health care benefits it offers employees. "In our engagement surveys," said O'Neel, "employees told us that they value our benefits, and wanted simplicity in their benefits, so we offer two core plans with excellent employee/employer cost ratios that have a broad array of coverage."

Businesses become more Shockproof when they realize that change is inevitable, and design their rewards accordingly. You don't need to look any further than the decline in the U.S. automotive industry for hard evidence of what happens when context changes and rewards don't. By maintaining 1970's era retirement benefits, tenure-driven work rules, and compensation levels that were driven by contract not performance, several of the most storied companies in the history of American business almost disappeared. The blame for this is neither all management's nor all organized labor's. Leaders from both camps tried for too long to adhere to an approach that was no longer effective, and their members and shareholders went along for the ride.

Even before the recession of the late 2000s, there was evidence of companies applying an adaptive approach to rewards. Whether through flexible benefits programs that allow employees more choice in selecting health care alternatives, or employee-driven career development plans where participants are accountable for charting their own careers, elements of flexibility have been part of rewards for some time. Similarly, it's well established that a company's salespeople are usually paid differently than its office staff or manufacturing personnel. Whereas some companies don't waver from a one-size-fits-all approach, Shockproof organizations realize that, in the case of rewards, form should follow function.

At times the bias for flexible, adaptive rewards is a matter of philosophy, but often it is driven by necessity. Seattle's Microsoft and many Silicon Valley high-tech firms were on the forefront of offering telecommuting, satellite offices, and flexible work hours, not just because they are "progressive employers," but because the unbearable traffic that followed their meteoric growth made them less attractive to the scarce talent that fueled their success. Technology itself was an enabler, as working remotely became easier and more commonplace. According to a December 2006 *BusinessWeek* article, at the time, 40 percent of IBM's workforce had no fixed office, as was the case for a third of AT&T's managers. Sun Microsystems, it reported, saved $400 million in real estate expenses over a six-year period by "allowing nearly half of all employees to work anywhere they want." Best Buy went a step further and implemented a flexible approach not only to where its office employees worked, but also when. This well-reported approach, called ROWE (for Results-Oriented Work Environment), has gone from an informal "guerilla" response to the challenges of maintaining work/life balance to "an official component of Best Buy's recruiting pitch."[19] It's not just that this kind of flexibility helps businesses succeed, it's the willingness to change rewards to

adapt to evolving business conditions that helps Shockproof
these organizations.

During the depths of the recession, we met some people from the Blind Industries and Services of Maryland who,
when forced to reduce their payroll, implemented an interesting take on furloughs. They called them "Do-Wop days"
which stands for "day off without pay." Sounds like fun,
right? The program requires every employee to take one day
off without pay every month (read, 5 percent payroll reduction); but employees schedule the day themselves, and for
this reason feel they are getting something in return. Faced
with this reality, employees used the days to extend week-
ends, run errands, and so forth. Interestingly enough, though
the program was implemented to close a budget gap, Do-
Wop days were so popular that the summer after they were
implemented many employees dropped by to inquire about
the program's return.

Meanwhile, back in the Seattle area, T-Mobile also
saw the need to adapt its rewards in response to changes in
the economy. Rather than take an axe to their programs, the
leadership team was deliberate in their approach. They froze
merit pay for all employees and, to guide other changes,
applied the same customer segmentation principles that
make T-Mobile successful. "In our call center environment,"
explained O'Neel, "we moved variable pay and put it in base
salary, and we still created a monthly incentive program for
which 40 percent of the population is eligible; and we main-
tained recognition awards programs for our over 30,000 frontline employees, and kept retail sales associate commissions
at prior levels," to provide some income protection for call
center employees and keep salespeople focused on revenue
generation. "Our rewards strategy is like our go-to-market
strategy," says O'Neel, "get 'em and keep 'em. Whether we

are targeting employees or customers, this approach decommoditizes our workforce and makes it clear that people are an important part of our strategy."

"We have the flexibility to adapt our measures," continues O'Neel, "but the key for us is not to change so much that people don't know what to focus on." While maintaining constant focus on call resolution and quality—"table stakes," O'Neel calls them—T-Mobile adapts its rewards to meet the realities of its call centers, where "coaching conversations and daily 'stand-up meetings' take place" and supervisors help their teams focus on current priorities, whether these are selling data plans, buy-one-get-one-free plans, or other promotions.

This level of flexibility contributes to Shockproofing T-Mobile because of the company's strong sense of the aforementioned two Cs of Alignment, *collaborate* and *cultivate*.

As we described in the January 2010 issue of WorldatWork's *workspan* magazine, Shockproof rewards are not for everyone, but in the hands of the right workforce and leaders they can play a major role in contributing to lasting success.[20]

> They have the most promise for employees and employers who are energized by change and the rewards of success. Organizations that treat their employees as commodities, and employees who view their work as "just a job," are not good candidates. Shockproof rewards rely upon high levels of affiliation and trust to create a mutually beneficial partnership between people and the enterprises where they work. These employers and employees ask "why not" more often than "why" and they have a bias for autonomy and experimentation, which

enables them to redeploy resources that would be
devoted to supervision and control in traditional
firms to generate higher returns.

## MAKING THE MOST OF YOUR MOST VALUABLE RESOURCE

The future belongs to those organizations that can manage
their talent (not carbon paper!) strategically. And if like those
leaders described in this chapter, they are strategic in how
they develop and reward their talent, these organizations will
be positioned to win consistently, over time. Shockproof talent management presents a great opportunity for leaders to
put existing tools to work in achieving new—and lasting—
results. By continually acquiring the right talent and deploying people to the right jobs, leaders set the stage for aligning
talent, the ultimate renewable resource, with strategy and
organization. Creating and maintaining this alignment is the
cornerstone of Shockproofing.

# CHAPTER 6

# Connections and Calibrations

The America's Cup is a race of management,
money, technology, teamwork, and last
and incidentally, sailing.
—Bill Koch, 1992 America's Cup winner

Yacht racing teams that win races like the America's Cup don't win simply because their boats have the most advanced design—although the design process is a highly scientific pursuit that optimizes structure, weight, and balance. And the team that wins doesn't always have the most qualified crew, though you won't find amateurs on board. The team that wins does so because they develop and expertly execute the strategy and tactics that are right for their particular yacht and crew. Since the weather during a race can't be predicted, especially over longer races, each team's strategy involves careful planning and anticipation of the potential conditions they may face and, importantly, how they plan to respond. Adaptability and responsiveness and how well the crew works together to make and execute decisions can make all the difference between winning and losing. It's an exercise in achieving and maintaining alignment.

## SHOCKPROOF COMPANIES MAINTAIN THE READY POSITION

In yacht racing it's the captain who assesses conditions, sets direction, and prepares the crew to navigate choppy waters. In business, leaders are responsible for creating and maintaining alignment. Getting it right requires carefully connecting strategy, organization, and talent, and then continually calibrating those connections in response to shocks and the anticipation of opportunities. The prize for creating and maintaining alignment is readiness. Companies that are

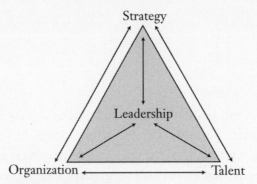

**Figure 6.1   The Shockproof Model**

Shockproof adopt a mind-set that is much like the posture of a tennis player, leaning forward and swaying on the balls of his or her feet in preparation to receive a serve. The point is to not get caught flat-footed.

Shockproof companies look ahead, beyond the next financial quarter. They care about short-term results but they are not trapped in a post-to-post management mentality, where they sacrifice longer-term growth and stability for short-term gains. Companies that achieve alignment can take advantage of opportunities and withstand significant shocks. Backhand. Forehand. Either way, they're ready. Creating alignment and knowing when to make dynamic adjustments to strategy, organization, or talent is the primary responsibility of leaders in Shockproof companies (see Figure 6.1).

## SHOCK HAPPENS. IT'S THE RESPONSE THAT COUNTS.

Mark Allan, CEO of UNITE Group, the company that provides student housing in the United Kingdom, describes the company's efforts to prepare for potentially challenging times in financial markets that they saw coming: "In our case it was a tightening of credit markets in 2001 and difficulty accessing funds to grow that was the initial warning sign, or mini shock.

It sparked the strategic review, informed our strategy, and caused us to redesign the organization. We didn't get there overnight, but we mapped out a clear path, aligned the resources, and brought our people with us."[1] It's a good thing the company's leaders were looking ahead in 2001, as UNITE's efforts to pursue joint ventures, rather than raise all of its own capital, and to create a unique investment fund in the student accommodation sector insulated the business effectively from the challenges associated with accessing capital during the much deeper recent global financial crisis that picked up steam in 2008. UNITE's focus on continuously aligning its organization with the evolving market, fine-tuning strategy, and sense-checking that the right people are in the right jobs contains an important thematic message: Align early, align often.

The fact of the matter is that in business, as in yacht racing, conditions change. Shock happens. Recent experience with the recession that started in 2008 provides us with a stark reminder. Maintaining alignment by calibrating the connections between strategy, organization, and talent acts as a highly effective shock absorber, as the UNITE Group Plc experience illustrates. Some companies anticipate shocks. They see them coming and make adjustments. Others get blindsided and fail to respond effectively, or quickly enough. In 2009, an astounding number of household company names outside of the financial services space declared bankruptcy, including GM, Chrysler LLC, Pacific Energy, BearingPoint Inc., Charter Communications Inc., Nortel Networks Inc., R.H. Donnelley Corporation, and General Growth Properties. This is the short list. Some of the companies that went bankrupt in 2009, especially in the auto industry, got caught flat-footed with unsustainable strategies and business models. Others were the victims of poor strategic planning or complacent leadership, and the recession simply pushed them over the edge or forced them to engage in the painful process of rebuilding out of the rubble.

The big Wall Street names like Citigroup took a massive hit because they were driving at 150 mph with no shock absorbers. While "putting the foot down" and taking the obvious risk might be acceptable on a German autobahn, it's turned out less than okay for the common investor, who paid dearly for the joyride, in lost retirement funds and increased taxation. Many of the big financial institutions simply weren't aligned. Their strategies and operations had become disconnected from each other and, some would argue, from reality. These firms became addicted to ridiculously high leverage, lax regulations, and cheap cost of capital. Leaders at many of these companies had allowed two of the essential requirements, or core capabilities, in financial services to be relegated in priority, in the pursuit of growth and profit. Risk management was an afterthought. Governance had borrowed the corporate jet and gone on vacation. The faster the traders and bankers drove the car and delivered profits, the more they got paid. Dizzying levels of profits had covered up huge misalignments and bloated organizations.

Shockproof businesses require a focus on core capabilities, governance, decision rights, and putting the right performance measures in place to keep things in balance and maintain alignment. All appear to have been insufficient. In the case of Citigroup, it appears that its balance sheet couldn't support the liquidity it needed or the size of the organization built around it. The response is still unfolding, but it involved shedding 55,000 employees in 2008 and another 57,700 in 2009, all after borrowing $45 billion from the government, which received a 27 percent stake in the company in return.[2] It's an extreme example but it illustrates what can happen when leadership fails to Shockproof a business, and leaders allow strategy, organization, and talent to get way out of whack with the external environment.

## DYNAMIC ADJUSTMENTS BUILD MUSCLE MEMORY

When Shockproof companies achieve alignment, things just feel right. The business achieves its objectives, employees feel connected to the strategy, and everyone is proud of the results. Regardless of size or market capitalization, or whether they are public or private, Shockproof companies demonstrate a level of alignment that allows them to thrive when times are good, and survive and rebound effectively when things get tough. Shockproof companies are not immune to setbacks, however. Well-known companies like Apple, Baxter, Pfizer, IBM, GE, and Starbucks have all taken a hit along the way; but when they do, they make the necessary adjustments and bounce back. What sets Shockproof companies apart is that they develop a "muscle memory," which is the key to their agility, adaptability, and resilience. The way they go about adjusting their strategies, their organizations, and talent management practices to create and maintain alignment strengthens and tones this muscle memory. It allows them to make adjustments and realign more rapidly and with less friction. Change is experienced by employees as a calibration instead of a violent knee-jerk reaction. Employees "get it." They spend less time reflecting on how things used to be and more time figuring out how to sync their efforts and capabilities with the new direction. Challenging market conditions can be overcome. Shocks are more easily absorbed because employees are directly connected to the strategy.

When misalignment exists, the opposite is true. Objectives are missed because targets are unrealistic. The organizational capabilities and talent needed to execute are lacking.

The organization design may not be fit for purpose, and people are not sufficiently engaged. They show up, they punch in, they get paid, and they go home. Leaders and managers describe the frustration of misalignment as similar to the experience of working a jigsaw puzzle without the box top. If you've ever tried it, you may have struggled to fill in the corners, then the outer frame, and eventually the middle pieces. And being human, especially as a kid, you probably decided to force-fit a few pieces together. When a company is not aligned, leaders and managers, in their efforts to make progress, often end up force-fitting projects or initiatives into the organization. On the face of it, the projects may seem to make sense, but never quite deliver the intended impact and results. People and functions seem at odds. For example, the marketing team's projects might not be in sync with what the sales force believes customers and prospects want to hear about. Or R&D may be developing highly engineered products with specifications and cost parameters far in excess of what customers will reasonably buy.

If strategy, organization, and talent are aligned in your company, chances are that you know it. And if you're a leader, you are probably doing your best to keep it that way. This requires vigilance. Leaders need to continuously scan for the first signs of misalignment and make swift adjustments to restore equilibrium.

## SERVING AN ACE

In tennis, opponents mix things up to disguise shots and throw each other out of position. The objective is to gain even the slightest competitive edge. Sometimes a player's serve provides such a competitive advantage that it is unreturnable.

Basically, whether the opponent is in the ready position or not doesn't matter. The server's placement of the ball, the speed at which it's delivered, the degree of spin, or all the variables combined make it impossible to return the serve. In business, leaders spend a lot of time trying to outwit, outrun, outmaneuver, or simply outlast their competitors. They sometimes try to win by putting together a better strategy. Other companies try to get an edge by hiring better talent. Better talent, logic would suggest, should be able to develop and execute a better strategy. Some companies ignore the competition and strive only to be their personal best. Other companies try to gain an advantage through how the organization is set up—matrixed, verticals, process-focused, functional orientation, self-directed work teams, practice areas, centers of excellence, centralized, decentralized. Feel free to add to the list.

What many companies miss is that creating and maintaining alignment between strategy, organization, and talent can deliver the unreturnable serve. An ace.

## Alignment's Competitive Edge

Outwardly, the "I'm a PC; and I'm a Mac" commercial, depicting an awkward conversation between a hip guy representing the Mac and a guy who looks like he doesn't get out much representing the PC, has come to symbolize the direct competition between Apple and Microsoft, where no holds are barred in pointing out speed, style, or performance superiority and deficits. It's fun to watch the competition. They go after each other. After all, anything to get an edge? Right? While the advertisement is thought-provoking, it's what's going on back at the ranch—particularly in Apple's case—that's more interesting.

Leaders, strategy, organization, and talent appear well aligned at Apple. Apple's television ads depict more than products. They convey a lifestyle and experience. The strategy is clear: Focus on delivering a superior user experience through a combination of innovative product design, Internet connectivity, entertainment, and media on the go. It's very compelling. It's also very profitable. The products look good, and they work. Creating iTunes was a master stroke. In February 2010, Apple surpassed the 10 billionth iTunes download; and its mobile devices, including iPods, iPhones, iPads, and MACs, continue to sell at 4G speed.[3] The iPad is practically a fashion accessory at the local coffee shop. Moreover, developers are getting in line to contribute to Apple's revenue stream by developing compatible applications for the App Store and related products. The simplest test of alignment or Shockproof credentials is whether or not the company is achieving its objectives. With 2009 revenues of $42.9 billion, net income of $8.2 billion, a strong product line, and multiple additional revenue streams, it appears Apple is achieving its financial objectives and pursuit of innovative product design.

Apple is, obviously, not totally immune to recessions and setbacks; it has experienced its ups and downs. In 2003, when many other technology companies were dealing with a slide in PC sales, Apple's quarterly profits likewise took a hit, sparking the company to make layoffs. The layoffs, however, were in areas like information systems, manufacturing, operations, and administration. It's noteworthy that there were no layoffs in engineering and product development, the areas that give Apple its competitive edge. Steve Jobs and Apple continued to hire talent in strategic functions. In 2003, he explained to *BusinessWeek*, "A lot of companies have chosen to downsize, and maybe that was the right thing for them. We chose a different path. Our belief was that if we kept putting great products in front of customers, they would continue to open their wallets. We've been turning out more new products than ever before."[4] The alignment between strategy and investments in talent is pretty clear, and it appears the decision has paid off. The foresight of leadership shouldn't go unnoticed either.

Apple has always controlled its own nuts-and-bolts hardware and operating platform, but now it's also controlling the content that ends up on its devices. Any application that makes it to the App Store requires approval by Apple. Some might say approval by "Big Apple," in a nod to a Big Brother level of controlling oversight. Since everything Apple does is focused on creating a superior consumer experience, it doesn't want to allow just any application to run on its devices. Quality control or profit control? You decide. Either way, it appears Apple is very clear about its strategy and has the talent needed to execute it, from product design through marketing.

Google is another company that appears to have achieved a very high degree of alignment between its strategy, organization, and talent. Of course Google's strategy is very different from Apple's. Google doesn't have any appetite for controlling other people's content. Google's mission is to organize the world's information and make it universally accessible and useful. Its business model essentially harvests significant dollars by providing a quick and easy pathway to other people's content. Its revenue mainly comes from the placement of ads on its own search engine using AdWords, its auction based advertising program, and on other web sites using its AdSense software. So Google takes a laissez-faire approach to content. While the quality of the content displayed is not managed by Google, the company has dramatically improved the efficiency at which individuals find the content they're looking for. It's hard to argue with the numbers. On revenues of $23.6 billion in 2009, Google delivered $6.5 billion in net income—or, a healthy 28 percent margin.[5]

At Google, employees are highly connected to the business, and have access to all sorts of amenities, from laundry to dry cleaning to high-end cafés, gaming rooms, and fitness centers. Why wouldn't employees stay at work and put in an extra few hours working to help the company achieve its mission? That's certainly what Google appears to be thinking. Attract the best, keep them engaged, and get the best out of them.

In March 2010, Google delivered on its threat to exit China—at least temporarily—in response to what the company cited as a serious hacking incident that amounted to "theft of intellectual property," in an article in the *Wall Street Journal* in January 2010.[6] The Chinese government's censorship of content was also an important issue for Google, and continues to be an ongoing source of conflict with the Chinese authorities. It's difficult to imagine Google over the long run advocating for freedom of information while simultaneously allowing the Chinese government to compromise that same principle through censorship. Sometimes, maintaining alignment requires sticking to your principles and convictions. When you say you believe in something, and that it's important to you, then it needs to be important to you all the time, not just when it's convenient. Expect ongoing dialogue between Google and the Chinese authorities.

When the Business Zigs Why Do the People Zag?[7]
—PETER V. LEBLANC

Sometimes, even all-stars drop a fly ball. Starbucks is seen as a company that sticks to its mission and treats its people well. It considers its *baristas* as extremely important employees—or *partners*, in the company's words—because of the work they do and their direct connection to customers. Benefits for part-timers, flex hours, autonomy—these are perks usually reserved for mid-level managers. The combination of good benefits, work environment, and probably a few espressos at the beginning of each shift have energized the frontline employees of Starbucks for decades. Starbucks is also known for asking for feedback and acting on suggestions from its baristas.

In 2009, nearly every industry was feeling the pinch of the deep recession, which trickled down to consumers like an overfilled latte with a dodgy lid. Spending $3.00 to $4.00 for a coffee, even if it is really good, became more than a lot of people were willing to fork over. The weight of overexpansion in good times, followed by the whiplash effect of the Great Recession; the continued assault by McDonald's; Dunkin' Donuts new affordable gourmet coffee lines; and grocery stores and chains seeking a piece of the action—all pushed Starbucks back on its heels. As a result, between 2008 and 2009, the company closed around 800 stores in the United States and about 100 overseas, and had to lay off 34,000 employees.[8] Tough decisions to make? No doubt. However, as a result of cost-cutting, Starbucks was able to increase its 2009 profits by 24 percent, to $390 million. Not too shabby.

During 2009, Starbucks made what appeared to be an unusual move by introducing instant coffee for sale in its stores. The company had apparently been exploring the instant coffee market for a long time. Leadership put their full support behind the new instant brew in a paper sleeve, known as VIA. Just add water.

What's a barista to think?

You can imagine the conversations that went on behind the counter. Baristas had been trained like curators to know their stuff. They know the origin of the beans; they know how the beans are carefully selected and blended. In the stores, most baristas seem to live the brand. They appear to be proud of the quality brews on offer, and customers enjoy chit-chatting with the pro who makes a flavorful, *fresh cup*. Prerecession, customers were more than willing to pay a premium for a handcrafted cup, poured by a barista who knew what he or she was doing.

Starbucks CEO Howard Schultz and his team launched a big push to encourage store employees to sell VIA. Baristas were trained on how to position the new product; but the expectations to hard-sell loyal customers on an instant coffee probably didn't sit all that well with how the baristas see their role. In fact, looking from the outside in, as a customer, it doesn't seem to fit that well with the company's positioning and value proposition. Isn't Starbucks focused on high quality, never bowing to mediocrity? Instant coffee somehow seems off the mark, even if it tastes good. So, are baristas pushing VIA? Maybe? Who knows? The point is, when the business zigs and there is even a remote chance that the people will zag in response, whatever leaders are trying to make happen will be an uphill battle. When something is off-kilter, or in the mind of employees doesn't quite match up with the value proposition as they understand it, or is contrary to how they see their role or the company, the result is misalignment. Misalignment is the enemy of productivity and results.

## YOU CAN'T LIP-SYNCH SUCCESS

There is no place in a Shockproof company for leaders who don't want to get their hands dirty and build a genuine understanding of the business. Taking it to the extreme, in the CBS television series *Undercover Boss*, C-suite leaders tried their hand at various jobs in their companies. Often posing as new hires, they worked alongside their unsuspecting front-line employees. In some cases, their efforts were judged by dedicated and committed coworkers as not up to par. They were provided with direct feedback about how they needed to improve. In the case of Larry O'Donnell, President and COO of Waste Management, he literally did get his hands dirty cleaning Porta Potties, sorting waste, and collecting garbage.[9] One thing that's clear in the series is that the leaders appear to gain a new sense of genuine appreciation for the efforts of their employees.

McDonald's has a strong track record of developing leaders, starting at the frontline, behind the counter taking orders or flipping burgers at the grill. McDonald's current CEO, Jim Skinner, many of its regional leaders, and the Dean of Hamburger University all started as restaurant crew. Ray Kroc's first grill man, Fred Turner, became CEO. Of McDonald's seven CEOs, four started as crew members. These leaders developed a visceral connection with the culture and operations of the company. Amazon.com founder and CEO, Jeff Bezos, did a stint at a McDonald's in Miami, during high school. In a 2001 *Fast Company* interview, when asked what he learned from the experience, and after joking about cracking lots of eggs efficiently with one hand, he said he learned something about customer service: "I learned that it's really hard. I was a cook. They wouldn't let me anywhere near the customers."[10] It appears he did learn a thing or two about customer service; he has mastered a focus on managing and informing customer preferences across all types of products at Amazon.com.

We are not suggesting that all CEOs need to start at the frontline; we're merely pointing out that the more they know about the business they are running, the better. Whether they learn it on their way up through the company or by actively engaging in what's going on, leaders must gain a perspective on the nuts and bolts of the business. In karaoke, it's easy to mimic Bono, or Gwen Stefani (though rarely both on the same night). You can prance around like a rock star, mumble your way through the lyrics, and almost pull it off—especially since no one is really paying attention. In Shockproof companies, there are no teleprompters or loud music to mask a lack of understanding or engagement in the business. There's a reason Apple rebounded when Steve Jobs returned, and that Starbucks got a jolt when Howard Schultz came back: They both have a visceral connection to their respective businesses. Upon his 2008 return, in a conference call, Schultz, who was the CEO from 1987 to 2000, committed to "reconnect the business to customers" by returning an "emotional attachment."[11] "We will deliver a consistent Starbucks experience that will be second to none," he said. He was also pragmatic about the challenge ahead when speaking to investors: "The reality we face is challenging and extremely exciting. There is no silver bullet and no overnight fixes." It seems like he was right.

There are other effective ways for leaders to stay connected with employees, to maintain alignment, and stay connected to daily operations. Engagement surveys can help get a pulse on the culture and level of employee commitment. But they're reactive. By the time leaders generate a meaningful response to the data, it's nearly always too late. Employees have likely moved on to new concerns or new jobs. Companies are beginning to embrace social media because they recognize that people today have a need for real-time information and interaction. It can prompt a more dynamic and inclusive conversation and provide a 360-degree perspective. By the time traditional newsletters or intranet sites post something, it's old news anyway. Employees are having today's conversation. The old news has already been sliced and diced into tweets and bytes. Today's conversation is the one that leaders need to stay connected to if they want to stay ahead of the game, learn what employees care about, and use the information to sense-check alignment and manage the zigs and zags.

With the level of transparency and scrutiny on leaders today, it's essential that they get their arms around the inner workings of their companies. Leaders need to understand decision-making processes and criteria that lead to both positive results and less favorable outcomes. Otherwise, it's difficult to establish and maintain alignment. It's amazing how little in-depth understanding leaders in financial services companies, under scrutiny after the 2008 meltdown, claimed to have about what's really going in their operations. If staying out of jail is the motivation, then hiding behind silos prevents acknowledgment of responsibility. Does it reflect appropriate governance and oversight? No. Granted, the highly engineered instruments like collateralized debt obligations most closely associated with the financial crisis are complex. We are not suggesting that a CEO should have a detailed technical understanding of exactly how the IT infrastructure is designed or how its security protocol is configured, for example. But in financial services firms, it seems reasonable to expect leaders to have a handle on the basics: how they make money.

## THE FIVE CS OF ALIGNMENT IN SHOCKPROOF COMPANIES

Over the past 30 years we have had the opportunity to work with and observe hundreds of companies and leaders across many industries and geographies that excel in creating alignment and executing strategy. We've also worked with companies that struggle to get it right. What we have found is that leaders in the most successful and resilient companies pay very close attention to what we refer to as the five Cs of alignment:

1. *Clarify:* Leaders clearly communicate the company's strategy and priorities so that all employees understand the link between what they do daily and the results achieved for customers, the business, and stakeholders.

2. *Collaborate:* Leaders, managers, and employees work together to execute on priorities and overcome challenges, because their interests are aligned.

3. *Cultivate:* Culture is carefully shaped by leaders and owned by employees to create an environment in which people can work together to achieve shared objectives and results.

4. *Concentrate:* Focus and disciplined execution on agreed-on priorities is practiced throughout the business. Flavor-of-the-month initiatives and distractions are avoided.

5. *Calibrate:* Leaders fine-tune the connections between strategy, organization, and talent in response to the external environment, to absorb shocks and capitalize on opportunities.

## A Thirst for Growth: The Five Cs in Action

If you happen to live in regions of the United States where the temperature can drop to minus 18 degrees Fahrenheit in winter, it's likely that you long for a temporary escape to a warmer climate from time to time. Perhaps your idea of that kind of vacation features a white sandy beach leading down to clear turquoise water. For over two decades, the beer commercials for Corona Extra have depicted the exact type of vacation that's often on people's mind in midwinter. While many of you might even have enjoyed a few Coronas yourselves, we'd guess that fewer of you are familiar with the company that's responsible for importing America's number-one imported beer. Crown Imports LLC, head-quartered in Chicago, is the operating company in a joint venture between Grupo Modelo and Constellation Brands Inc., that imports, distributes, and markets the Modelo portfolio and other beer brands across the entire United States, including Corona Extra, Corona Light, Modelo Especial, Negra Modelo, Pacifico, St. Pauli Girl, and the Tsingtao beer brands.

In the second quarter of 2009, led by Bruce Jacobson, Executive Vice President of Sales, Crown Imports embarked on a significant initiative to transform its overall go-to-market strategy and sales organization. The economic downturn that the U.S. economy had experienced, coupled with a belief that it would rebound as it had from all previous downturns, was a key motivation. "Essentially," Jacobson said, "the organization had experienced a sustained period of continued growth for some 15 years, based on the strength of our brands and our culture. When we doubled the size of the company overnight and, at the same time, had to deal with a marketplace in which our business growth reversed, we needed to do something differently"[12] Jacobson said his instincts and the numbers led him to believe it was time for significant change. "We were determined to do some things in 2009 that would help us in a tough economy, but also lay the foundation for accelerated growth once the economy recovered. We couldn't afford to waste the opportunity when times were difficult to step back and figure out how to set ourselves up for success," explained Jacobson. Crown Imports made a commitment to Shockproof the organization. The entire initiative was aimed at aligning strategy, organization, and talent to drive profitable growth.

Besides having an effective advertising campaign that has made Corona synonymous with relaxing at the beach, there's a lot of work that goes into importing, marketing, and distributing America's leading imported beer. During the transformation at Crown Imports, leaders took the time to *clarify* the company's strategy, the competitive landscape, the importance of the company's brands, and the day-to-day execution priorities for employees.

As Bill Hackett, President of Crown Imports, explained, there is greater complexity to this business than a consumer might imagine: "Firstly, our brands are sold in multiple channels both on-premise, in bars, restaurants, and hotels, and off-premise in national chain stores and grocery and convenience stores.[13] Managing brand positioning is a key focus area, according to Hackett: "Making sure that our brands are effectively positioned and represented in multiple markets and channels requires a well-thought-through strategy and consistent, effective execution." Competition is stiff, meaning it's vitally important to have something unique to offer. "We have to compete for the attention of a wholesaler tier that is being pulled in many directions by multiple competitors: the major domestic beers, other imports, and craft beers," added Hackett. Getting mindshare and real collaboration with customers requires a lot of effort. "We are also positioned at one of the highest price points in the category, so getting attention and commitment to our brands requires real differentiation," he said.

Hackett is a strong believer that strategy, organization, and talent must be aligned, and that having leaders who can *calibrate* the three is the key to winning. "The right strategy is important," he said, "but it's imperative that we have the right processes and structure to get the job done. That is also why we work hard at hiring the best talent in the market. We need people who are focused on winning, every day. Success in this business is all about having the right game plan and the right people to execute it." Hackett spends a lot of time thinking about how to *cultivate* Crown Imports' culture, because he sees it as a key source of competitive advantage, "A critical element of our formula and, I believe, the underlying reason for our success to date is our culture. We like to say that we take our business seriously but we don't take ourselves too seriously," said Hackett. "In our business we have a culture that supports our people. Our success is about the success of our people. We invest in their development and support their wins. We've always had good people who understand the beer business and come to work every day to make a difference," he continued.

Leaders at Crown Imports engaged the sales organization in providing their perspective on what was working well and where they saw opportunities for improved collaboration to drive results. Jacobson said, "Consistent with our belief that it's our people in the field who interact with distributors and customers on a daily basis that have the most valuable insights about our business, it only made sense to tap into their thinking."

The sales force didn't hold back in providing their feedback and insights, confirming leadership's view about how passionate they are about the business. A data-driven, fact-based review of current and anticipated market dynamics was also conducted. Among other variables, market share versus advertising spending, population growth trends in the target consumer demographic, and anticipated economic recovery were analyzed. According to Jacobson, "It was really important for us to make decisions based on a complete fact base. Taking such a rigorous approach to analyzing the market and our channels provided us with the confidence to make resource allocation and organization design decisions that may otherwise have been difficult."

The company's leaders were determined to get it right. It was essential that the strategy and go-to-market approach be clear from the C-suite to the Market Development Managers. They focused their attention on the following questions:

- Do we have a clear strategy for each channel and customer segment?

- Have we established the right priorities to foster collaboration and drive results?

- How do we sustain our culture of passion for the brands, high performance, and individual and team success?

- How do we ensure concentration and disciplined focus on the initiatives, activities, and results that matter most?

- Will the proposed organization structure support efficient decision making and consistent, timely execution?

- Do we have the right people in the right roles to align our overall strategy with day-to-day activities in the field?

Achieving strategic clarity is not just a numbers game at Crown Imports. Jacobson recalled that answering these questions required combining multiple years of leadership insight and knowledge about the industry with the data. "Relying on solid data allowed us," he said, "to remove much of the emotion typically associated with broad-based changes to the organization. We made the decisions with the end in mind. Where did we need to be from a business standpoint? That was the question we focused on answering."

Ultimately, Crown Imports is a consumer-driven brand. From Hackett's perspective, changes to the organization were focused "on improving how resources were allocated to ensure that the portfolio of brands and, therefore, the business, is positioned for short- and long-term success." The initiative was focused on being cost-neutral, versus cutting costs. "Reducing costs was not the objective," said Jacobson, "the change was about placing the right bets in the right markets."

Hackett, who describes himself as a very results-focused leader, pointed out that, "Bruce [Jacobson] and his team established detailed performance expectations with well-defined metrics. Career paths were developed so people can see exactly what they need to do to reach the next level."

Hackett also believes that once a strategy is in place, "getting the right level of focus, and to ensure that people *concentrate* on the initiatives and priorities that drive results, is essential." Reflecting on the work the team completed, Hackett notes, "This business continues to be increasingly competitive, so we needed to give ourselves every edge possible. I think what we have now is a more efficient go-to-market approach that focuses our people on the right activities, where they can have the greatest impact on the business, grow the portfolio's share of market, and advance their own growth, personally and professionally."

At the end of the project Jacobson commented that if they had tried to tackle it internally, they "would have started the initiative where we ended up 90 days in: with the organization chart." In this case, as in most, starting with the strategy and the market, thinking about the work that needs to get done, and the capabilities and processes needed to support it, led to the right organization structure.

According to Hackett, the changes were made during a period "when we just had to deliver results. We couldn't afford to press pause on the business to make it happen. We had to execute the change plan, while delivering results. As they say, 'We crossed the channel and burned the boat.'" Jacobson believes that the "changes were made at the right pace to ensure enough deliberation and effective decision making." Also, having the leaders involved and on board early "improved the quality of decision making, and we had their buy-in all along," he said.

In communicating the change to the sales organization and its functional partners in Marketing, Finance, and HR, Jacobson stressed the necessity for speed and agility, along with the need to *collaborate* across channels effectively. "We are a relatively small company, in terms of headcount. However, we used to be small and *slow*. Slow in decision making and change. People really got it when we said that being small and slow is never a good place to be. The reality is that we will continue to be relatively small; but if we are going to be small, we need to be *nimble*." To achieve that, Crown moved from eight geographically focused divisions with a high degree of centralized decision making to four fully functional business units with far greater decision latitude, and the P&L responsibility and accountability that comes with it. The new structure is designed to maximize collaboration across channels, within each business unit, by having fewer points of contact from a communications standpoint and a business unit leader who coordinates the effort of selling resources across channels.

Looking back on the most challenging aspects of the change, Bill Hackett, who likes to take a hands-on approach to the business, said, "I stayed out of the way and let Bruce [Jacobson] and his team do the work." Hackett demonstrates a high level of self-awareness. "Knowing that the process was outside of my direct purview was painful, but I put a lot of faith in Bruce's commitment and passion to making it work." As for Jacobson, he said it was the aspect of "managing people through the changes, and communicating the rationale, especially for individuals who were not an appropriate fit within the new go-to-market strategy" that proved difficult for him. He also highlighted one of the most rewarding aspects of the initiative: "We put several people in stretch roles, and they are working their tails off and showing really good progress. They've stepped up."

The go-to-market strategy and organizational changes were announced in December 2009 and implemented in the first quarter of 2010. Crown Imports' efforts have started to pay off. The 2009, year-end sales volume, measured in cases, was down by approximately 4 percent, while the case volume trend in March through June of 2010 had turned around and was in positive territory by approximately 3.5 percent.

## ZOOMING IN ON THE FIVE Cs OF SHOCKPROOF ALIGNMENT

### Clarify

The first ingredient in creating a Shockproof organization is to *clarify* the company's strategy and what's required to execute it. In an earlier example, Steve Jobs and Apple were determining where to make layoffs and realize cost savings in 2003, and they made the right call. They knew how Apple creates value. Administration, operations, and IT are needed to run a company, but customers don't care about the internal plumbing of an organization; that's not why they part with their dollars. It's the products that open wallets. When companies get clear about strategy and how they are differentiated from competitors, they can focus on the right priorities. Even when making tough decisions, like layoffs, strategic clarity can extend, or at least maintain, competitive edge.

Leaders at Crown Imports know what drives their success and profitability. Simply knowing what matters most, however, is no cause to crack open a beer and celebrate. They recognize that unless everyone in the company is thirsty for the same results, and focused on the same priorities, they are unlikely to achieve their growth objectives. That's why they break down their strategy into clear priorities for each channel and get their people focused on execution.

Clarifying the strategy is not about the pithy poster on the wall in the lobby of the corporate office, with the mission, vision, and values neatly lined up. That's not to say that they're not important. Getting clear about the activities that create value and support strategy execution is what's important, and yet this clarity is lacking at so many companies.

At PricewaterhouseCoopers (PwC), the firm's leadership is very clear about the strategy and what creates value. Leaders focus their energy on aligning the entire firm with the strategy. The firm is "built and sustained over the long term based on the quality of the relationships that we establish and grow with clients, and the quality of our work," according to John Carter, PwC's Chief Administrative Officer. He adds, "This may sound simple, but it's surprising how many organizations can get distracted by internal issues like reporting relationships or the performance metrics that are in place."[14] During difficult economic times it's even more important to PwC to carefully manage its client relationships. "All firms in our industry experienced fee pressure as our clients attempted to deal with the harsh down cycle," said Carter. "We made commitments to invest in relationships, because over the course of the firm's history strong client relationships have been the key ingredient to our success."

Similarly, Bob Irwin, CEO at Sterling Commerce, believes "clarity requires communicating what the company is focused on and, in equal measure, what it's not focused on."[15] Leaders need to simplify the complex. As Irwin puts it, "You need to break things down for people and create a connection to what they do every day. It's equally important to highlight what you're not going to focus on as it is to communicate the key areas of focus."

At PwC, everyone from partners to newly hired associates see the value of a client service mentality. As Carter reflects, "Unlike technology or software companies that make money while they sleep, our value is delivered by our people collaborating with clients to tackle difficult business problems and recommend solutions. This places a responsibility on everyone in the firm to ensure that we are managing relationships effectively and bringing our best and brightest talent to serve our clients." And he notes, "Our mission and strategy couldn't be much clearer."

Strategic clarity and alignment occur when leaders set direction and reinforce the rationale for the chosen direction. It's about staying on message. In politics, staying on message is about being consistent, even if it's irritating to watch a politician on television deflect a tough inquiry and instead respond with his or her message without answering the question that has been asked. Frustrating to the viewer, yes, but the politician effectively gets his or her point across. In business, leaders who are consistent are easier to follow. Leaders need to paint a picture that shows how success will be achieved, and reinforce the right activities.

While large firms like PwC, or companies like IBM or GE, may have a clear sense of purpose, the complexity arises in the fact that they are truly global. PwC, for example, operates in 151 countries with approximately 160,000 employees. Achieving clarity across the entire firm about the mission and strategy is easier said than done; but, according to Carter, the firm's "collective experience, leadership, and capabilities make a difference. We know what's important and we make sure everyone in the firm is on the same page."

**Zooming Out to Clarify**   When we work with leadership teams on strategy clarification and implementation, we encourage them to step back, *zoom out* and then *zoom in* again before focusing on how the company *really* creates value. Sometimes, it's hard to get leaders fully aligned around the priorities for their business. Why? Because they lead different functions; or they might have built their careers in different companies; or they come from different industries. In other situations, they simply have a different interpretation of what's important. What's interesting is that these differences in opinion occur even when the strategy seems crystal clear on paper.

Creating alignment goes far beyond agreeing on the right strategy for the business. The strategy has often been signed off by the board for months, before we are invited to the table, in which case it's not up for debate. What is up for debate is how to implement it. This requires setting priorities. Resources are finite. Prioritization requires choices. Not all the initiatives typically proposed by leaders will have the same impact on the business. Some will deliver short-term results. Other investments are aimed at delivering ROI over a two- to three-year horizon. All of a sudden getting an agreement about how to execute strategy can be challenging.

**I Think I Lost You. Wait . . . Wait . . . Can You Hear Me Now?** We think it's a safe bet that most readers own a mobile device or PDA, so we'll present the example of a wireless telecommunications service provider to illustrate the process we sometimes use to build strategic clarity and gain leadership alignment. Think Verizon, AT&T, T-Mobile, Vodafone, Orange. Ask yourself the question, *What do I really care about when picking a service provider for my mobile phone or PDA?* Jot down the first three things that come to mind.

Now imagine for a moment that you have just walked into the boardroom of a leading wireless telecommunications company. You are right in the middle of a leadership alignment meeting. Leaders are standing up, sharing their opinions vigorously, and highlighting boxes on charts that hang on the wall. They clearly don't agree on which boxes are most important, but they seem more than happy to debate and advocate for their own perspectives. A few of the leaders are pulling up spreadsheets they prepared ahead of time to help make their cases.

Two weeks before the meeting everyone received the latest version of the strategy document. They all read it carefully before they arrived at the meeting. Some underlined key themes. Others turned down page corners or made notes.

A month prior to the meeting, each leader had a one-on-one conversation with the consulting team to discuss what they believe are the most critical capabilities, processes, activities, and initiatives to drive long-term profitable growth. The chart on the wall is the result of those conversations, a detailed analysis of the strategic plan and the prior year's operational plans. It's called a *value tree* (see Figure 6.2). It's a graphical map with connecting branches that all lead back to sustainable, profitable growth. Everything that appears to the right influences, or drives, the outcomes on the left side of the value tree.

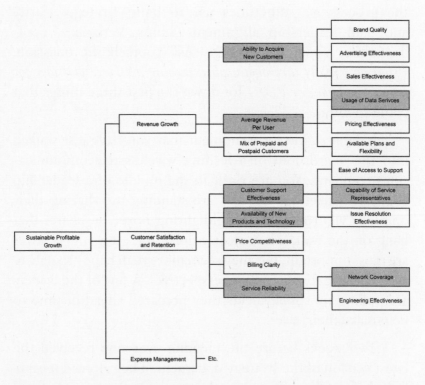

**Figure 6.2    Sample Value Tree for a Wireless Telecommunications Service Provider**

Now, back in the boardroom, real time. You notice that some of the leaders are anxiously leafing through the strategy document, with one eye focused on the action going on at the wall, where a handful of leaders are standing and engaging in a spirited dialogue. The facilitator is asking questions:

- What factors influence or drive sustainable profit-able growth?

- What drives customer satisfaction and retention?

- What drives average revenue per user?

It takes a while, but after reviewing some detailed analyses on customer churn rates, satisfaction scores, and average monthly revenue and profits, eventually leaders agree on the highest-priority areas on which they should focus. You're glad to see that what you most care about attracts a lot of agreement. It's service reliability! *Does my phone work and do calls stay connected or get dropped?* You're surprised that connection speed for your smartphone doesn't show up, but then you notice that it is captured as part of service reliability.

Next, the leaders review the proposed operational plans and investments for each functional area against the backdrop of the priority areas they just agreed on. You observe that some of the initiatives and investments get a green light pretty quickly, whereas others are pushed to the side. Bandwidth upgrades get an almost unanimous vote. More analysis is requested by the COO to see if upgrading the IT infrastructure in the contact center will deliver the expected returns and improvements to customer service levels.

After lunch, the meeting reconvenes and the COO leads a discussion about the key areas on which leaders agreed to focus. They are looking at a matrix, which they are calling an

| Key Result Areas | Drivers | Performance Measures | Initiatives |
|---|---|---|---|
| Customer Satisfaction and Retention | Customer Support Effectiveness:<br>• Ease of access to support.<br>• Capability of service representatives.<br>• Issue resolution effectiveness. | • Percentage of issues resolved first pass.<br>• Average call wait time.<br>• Speed of issue resolution.<br>• Average call handle time. | • Service representative sourcing plan.<br>• Representative on-boarding.<br>• Web-based training.<br>• Project "single screen."<br>• Incentive dial. |
| Revenue Growth | • Ability to acquire new customers.<br>• Ability to retain customers. | • Number of new activations per month.<br>• Average revenue per user.<br>• Customer churn rate. | • "Win to connect."<br>• Customer pulse.<br>• Project "win back." |

**Figure 6.3    Execution Matrix**

*execution matrix* (see Figure 6.3). On the left side of the matrix the key result areas are listed; the high-priority drivers appear directly to the right, in the next column. Performance measures linked to the drivers are also captured. Farthest to the right are the projects and initiatives that were debated earlier. Some have an asterisk beside them indicating they require further analysis. Others got the green light, before lunch.

The meeting ends. Your brief window into leadership alignment at the wireless service provider is closed, but it gets you thinking. You think about how effectively the leaders at the meeting mapped the connections between capabilities, processes, and people back to the goal of sustainable profitable growth. You also liked the idea of the execution matrix, which really cemented in your mind the links between value drivers, performance measures and initiatives. You think to yourself, *"Achieving this degree of clarity and alignment at the leadership level looks like a recipe for success."*

**Creating Clarity and Alignment versus Declaring It**   Creating strategic clarity and alignment requires genuine collaboration by leaders, as described in the example of the telecommunications company. If you've recently participated in a strategic or operational planning session where it felt as if everybody was pushing his or her own personal agenda, you know how difficult it can be to get alignment and set priorities that the entire leadership team can agree on. When it feels like your colleagues on the leadership team are not really listening to your perspective, not really engaging to understand each other's views, it can be pretty frustrating. You may also have been in situations where the meeting has already happened "outside the room" and the planning session is simply a formality, or worse, a charade, not really intended to get everyone's perspective and build alignment.

In Japan, the prevailing business practice is that before the formal meeting, participants have already drawn conclusions and made up their minds about the information to be presented at the meeting. They have a term they use to describe the process, *nemawashi*. Nemawashi means, literally, "to dig around the roots" in order to prepare a plant for transplant. Without proper nemawashi, a bonsai tree, for example, when transplanted to new soil may die. When used in a business context, it implies doing some groundwork ahead of time. It's expected. Nemawashi is not a bad thing, as long as it's inclusive. In the United States, and elsewhere for that matter, putting in a little groundwork can be a good idea, especially to prepare for a challenging decision, or one that has significant or potentially controversial implications. Perhaps you have been asked to "socialize" an idea with a peer or stakeholder before a meeting? Starting a meeting with 8 to 10 people and not having prior insight into their perspectives on an important issue beforehand is often the recipe for a very long day on the winding road to alignment.

Clarifying strategy and how to achieve it is fundamental to creating a Shockproof business. Getting leaders to agree on strategy is one thing; getting them aligned on exactly how to execute it is an entirely different proposition. In the absence of strategic clarity, most leaders and managers will focus on what they believe are the right things to do. If you've got really good talent, that may not seem like such a bad thing. They probably won't stray too far from the things that create value for the business. However, even the best leaders will sometimes deviate from what adds value, thereby reducing productivity and execution effectiveness. Think about the multiplicative effects of 30,000 employees doing their best but all deviating to some degree or another from what really matters most because they are unclear about what that is. Does the word *shockprone* ring a bell?

## Collaborate

In a Shockproof company the relationship between strategic clarity and collaboration is one of symbiosis. They feed off each other. With greater clarity comes easier collaboration. Greater collaboration fosters improved clarity. Once strategic clarity is established, leaders can turn their attention to how they *collaborate*. That's why Shockproof companies constantly seek to clarify and confirm strategic direction. They get the right leaders involved in the conversation. The quality and frequency of the conversations, even if they merely confirm the direction they are already taking, leads to greater clarity and paves the way for collaboration. Constantly seeking and confirming strategic directions is not paranoia. Rather, it's the preemptive antidote to complacency. Complacency, as we know, is an important milestone on the road to becoming shockprone. In his recent book *How the Mighty Fall: And Why Some Companies Never Give In*, Jim Collins points to the fact that "hubris born of success," can put your company on a slippery slope.[16]

Collaborating to execute strategy is essential. When leaders are on the same page about the processes, capabilities, technology, and talent needed to execute, they are well down the path toward alignment and becoming more Shockproof. One of the benefits of using a tool and process like the value tree, which we introduced earlier, is that it's a "pure" representation of what's needed to execute strategy. It's not organized to align with or to reflect functional areas. It's not a P&L turned sideways, either. As a result, it allows leaders to look at the business from a fresh, objective perspective. It takes leaders out of their functional silos and encourages them to think about the business in a more holistic manner. This type of thinking is important in building collaboration.

The leaders at the Martin Agency, introduced in Chapter 5, are absolutely clear about their strategy, which is centered on creating strong relationships with clients, deploying talent effectively, and ensuring team collaboration and accountability for the quality of the work. Account teams are called "ownership teams" for a reason. Each team member is held accountable for the same performance measures. John Adams, the Martin Agency's Chairman and CEO, explains, "The Account Executive is held accountable for the quality of the creative work, and the Creative Director is tied to the financial success of the account. When we review performance, we look at several measures for the entire team, including quality of work, team morale, client relationship, financial health, and idea generation and innovation."[17]

Collaboration, as elected officials in Congress say, creates the need "to reach across the aisle." In the example of the wireless telecommunications provider, it requires several functions and leaders to collaborate and focus their combined efforts on significant drivers of value such as:

- Achieving *customer satisfaction and retention* requires HR to source and hire capable service reps, and Operations to run an effective contact center.

- *Service reliability* requires Finance and Engineering to collaborate and assess the level of capital investment needed to expand and maintain a reliable network that provides good coverage.

In Shockproof companies, leaders build relationships and networks of influence and connections to get things done. We all know that the names of people in the boxes on the organization chart depict the formal route; but in most companies, having the right relationship in different functions at any level can grease the skids and facilitate collaboration.

## Cultivate

When appropriately cultivated, culture can act like the sinew that supports the muscle memory of Shockproof companies. Conversely, culture can also be the Achilles' heel of the shock-prone. Certain types of culture can make it difficult for companies to adapt and change. Leaders who have figured out how to create, shape, and reinforce culture are able to achieve, and sustain, higher performance levels, and also withstand shocks. Culture evolves and is shaped over time. It clearly doesn't happen overnight, and leaders can't *declare* a culture and expect to it occur.

At technology companies and consumer electronics companies that rely heavily on new products and services, a culture of innovation is fostered and encouraged. The culture encourages people to always be thinking about how to innovate products and services, how to create something new and of value to the end user. At Apple, for example, Steve

Jobs places a relentless focus on design innovation. Apple is very single-minded in its commitment to create an unparalleled consumer experience. As Jobs puts it, "Innovation has nothing to do with how many R&D dollars you have. When Apple came up with the Mac, IBM was spending at least 100 times more on R&D. It's not about money. It's about the people you have, how you're led, and how much you get it."[18]

Innovation at Apple happens through continuously pushing and testing boundaries and new ideas. "When a good idea comes," said Jobs, "you know, part of my job is to move it around, just see what different people think, get people talking about it, argue with people about it, get ideas moving among that group of 100 people, get different people together to explore different aspects of it quietly, and, you know—just explore things."[19]

In professional service firms like PwC, maintaining and sustaining a client service culture is all the more challenging when the average employee tenure is four to five years. "While we have a long and rich foundation of client service, we need to manage that focus and culture carefully and instill it in new hires continuously," said John Carter, PwC's CAO. This places a real onus on leaders to take a "long-term view on almost everything we do and to ingrain that way of thinking in our people and culture," he believes. When PwC is making decisions about the firm's people, for example, the multigenerational impact on the business, its people, and culture are considered. "We need to assess the impact on current partners, on recent hires who aspire to be partners, and on retired partners who are paid from current-year profit versus a pension fund," Carter explained. This multigenerational responsibility, he continued, is a "reminder of our responsibility and stewardship role as leaders, and helps ensure that the longer-term view is balanced with the shorter-term perspective."

According to Carter, the firm has a highly collaborative leadership team and culture that "brings multiple and diverse perspectives to the table, to focus on everything from increasing the services offered to current clients to increasing market penetration to improving our bottom line." This collaborative decision-making culture "gets the right people in the room, asking the right questions, and ultimately making the decisions that link the efforts of our people to the firm's future," he added. Clearly, the culture of client service and collaboration at PwC is an outcome—an outcome of "how leaders lead, how they interact with clients, how client work gets managed and executed, how people are developed, what's reinforced and rewarded," said Carter.

**Culture Change at "Big Blue"**   Getting one person to change can be difficult. Changing an established culture in an organization can be even more challenging, even when it's exactly what's needed. There are numerous examples of companies whose leaders have identified as a business imperative the need to change the culture. They've recognized that unless the culture changes it's highly unlikely that the business will succeed. When technology industry outsider Lou Gerstner took the reins as CEO at IBM, the company was in a world of hurt—what many would call an outright crisis. In 1993, IBM reported an $8.1 billion net loss. By the time Lou Gerstner stepped down in March 2002, IBM had reestablished itself; he had firmly put the company back on the map. He left IBM with 65,000 more employees than when he took the reins, and a 2001 profit of close to $8 billion. Gerstner claimed that the extent of the crisis gave him the platform to make broad sweeping changes. Early in his tenure, he was apparently very open, direct, and fact-based in conversations with employees. According to William J. Cook of *U.S. News & World Report*, Gerstner told his team, "Look, guys, we've lost $16 billion in the last three years; *Fortune* magazine says we're a dinosaur. Don't you think we ought to change? I mean, it's pretty obvious what we're doing ain't working."[20]

In a 2008 speech at Georgetown University, and looking back at the challenge he had undertaken at IBM, Gerstner spoke about changing the company's culture as one of the most important elements underpinning the successful turn-around that he led. The most critical ingredient of transformation, Gerstner proposed, is the role of corporate culture. He discussed the need to integrate IBM's business units into a single, unified company, and reward the right behaviors. He spoke about the need to maintain past cultural strengths while eliminating rules that had lost their relevance. "Management can only create the environment," he said, "and then invite the workforce to change its culture."[21]

## *Concentrate*

Focus and discipline are more than buzzwords in Shockproof companies. Shockproof companies clarify what it is they intend to do, set priorities, collaborate to achieve the priorities, and stay focused. They actively avoid and fend off distractions. When new initiatives are proposed, leaders question which initiatives should come off the plate, to free up or redirect resources and people to execute. They also assess and prioritize initiatives based on the extent to which they extend their competitive advantage.

Bob Irwin notes that early in his tenure as CEO at Sterling Commerce, prior to developing the strategy for the business with his leadership team, industry analysts that covered the company's products and services would frequently make suggestions and ask questions about the direction the business was headed: "Bob, have you considered this adjacency or potential application?" The analysts frequently offered valuable perspectives, so Irwin found himself responding by acknowledging the "interesting suggestions or idea." Once the strategy was developed, however, he noticed he was not only acknowledging suggestions but also being much clearer about "what's in and what's out," based on the strategy.

To maximize focus and maintain alignment, Irwin realized he was starting to say no. "Saying no to suggestions that may be interesting but that are ultimately a distraction from the strategy is part of my role," according to Irwin. Saying no in this context, Irwin was quick to point out, "is not stifling innovation. It's merely narrowing the focus of attention to align [everyone's] effort with the strategy." Irwin also pointed out that, "Innovation and new ideas are essential and welcomed, as long as they align with or extend current capabilities or products that fall within our strategy. Achieving growth is already challenging, so given the size of our market share, it's much easier to grow share in something we already know how to do than to chase every new idea." Irwin clearly believes that his "role as CEO is to continue to reinforce the strategy and make sure that everyone, from Dublin, Ohio, to Bangalore, India, is clear about the priorities" for the business.

The low-fare, no-frills European airline Ryanair has achieved cult status for relentless concentration on cost-cutting and penny-pinching. Ryanair's CEO, Michael O'Leary, might not last too long in the politically correct boardrooms of the United States, but a lot of CFOs would like to be on his team due to his maniacal focus on cost-cutting and profitability and his determination to see off the competition. Commenting on the recent economic downturn, he said, "We need a recession. We have had 10 years of growth. A recession gets rid of crappy loss-making airlines, and it means we can buy aircraft more cheaply."[22] Incidentally, there are no seat-back pockets on Ryanair's airplanes. Why not? It reduces aircraft turnaround time and cleaning costs at the gate, since there is no trash to remove or airline magazines or safety cards to replenish for the next passengers. And O'Leary got the kind of publicity he enjoys when he suggested—not for the first time—in January 2010 that Ryanair was pushing ahead with plans to begin charging passengers a £1 or €1 to use the onboard toilets. He claimed, of course, that it was a cost-cutting initiative. If passengers didn't use the toilets as much, fewer would be needed on board, allowing for more seats to be installed. The additional revenues then could be used to lower seat costs for passengers. Okay, we get it, loud and clear: Ryanair is aligned around being a low-cost airline.

In his Georgetown speech, Lou Gerstner also pointed to the need to stay focused on the company strategy and to ignore distractions. He suggested that one of the most important decisions he made was to ignore the investment bankers and others who were calling for the breakup of the company. He rebuilt IBM around its core capability of understanding technology and moved toward providing end-to-end integrated services. The services were aimed at solving business problems and facilitating improved efficiency. The portfolio of services included consulting on the design of corporate IT systems to running a company's e-commerce capability.

Gerstner also spoke of the temptation to move off strategy. "I have seen so many companies that, when the going gets tough in their base business, decide to try their luck in new industries. You have to be selective in the business you choose," he noted. "I have learned that this problem is the most common cause of corporate mediocrity." Importantly, Gerstner said he believed all strategies are similar because all industries share a set of basic conditions that are understood by all the players. If that's the case, what makes the difference? In his perspective, "Execution is the most unappreciated skill in business leaders."

## *Calibrate*

**For Every Zig There's a Zag**   Dynamically adjusting the connections between strategy, organization, and talent is the most important principle in creating and sustaining a Shockproof business. It's also one of the hardest to pull off. There is no pause button, so adjustments need to be made carefully. Some compare this process to changing a plane's engines midflight. Many leaders fail to fully appreciate the effect that even small changes can have on an organization and its people. They believe that they can isolate and make a small tweak in one element without causing a ripple effect in others. That's almost never the case. Small changes in strategy, structure, governance, business processes, performance metrics, and rewards all cause significant knock-on effects. The ripple effects occur in part because of the intended change, but equally because of the assumptions and perceptions that people have relating to the change. That's why change management is so critical.

Kevin Boyle, of Boyle & Associates in Corvallis, Oregon, spent a significant portion of his career working with the Communications Workers of America (CWA) and the International Brotherhood of Electrical Workers (IBEW) at Pacific Northwest Bell, US WEST (later, Qwest), helping leaders from management and unions understand the systemic nature of change and the dynamics that occur within and between companies and unions. One day, after what he described as "several difficult labor-management meetings," he returned home, vented, and shared his frustration with his son, Ben, who was 14 at the time. "I was having real difficulty getting people to see the systemic nature of their union and company organizations and the impact of their decisions and actions," said Boyle.[23] His son, who Boyle says is very creative, came up with an idea. "Together, we built a mobile, similar to what you might see in a child's room," said Boyle. The mobile was built to show two independent organizations, the company and the union. It consisted of several colored discs, each individually labeled: structure, governance, decision rights, performance measures, communications, and rewards. Each disc represented a different aspect of the organization. "When all the discs are hanging in the right place, it's in perfect balance," explained Boyle. "Adjust or remove one element in either organization and immediately a ripple effect occurs across both systems. The entire system becomes temporarily unbalanced as it veers out of alignment." It's a powerful visual aid, and a reminder to leaders of the responsibility to think through the potential unintended effects of planned changes across organizations. Changes to strategy, organization, or talent often require calibrations to restore alignment.

If calibrations are difficult to pull off, imagine what an overhaul requires. The recording industry is still trying to get clear about how to change its business model in response to digital music distribution. In instances like this, the need for change requires more than realigning talent to fit a new strategy, or making an adjustment in how people do work. The degree of change and realignment likely required for the music industry to bounce back is wholesale. It would seem that the recording industry has not just been shocked, but is reeling from electrocution. Sony, Warner Music, EMI, and Universal, known as the "big four," have been cost-cutting beyond their cores. EMI's recorded music division has shrunk by almost half since 2001.[24] Meanwhile, a senior industry executive reports that only one recording artist will make money for his record company. Sony Music analysts reported that the only CD sales that made them any money in 2009 hinged primarily on the death of Michael Jackson, which led to "record" sales.[25]

Changes in how people want to experience music have led to growth in the live music sector, making it even harder to make a buck from recorded music. Prince gave away CDs to everyone who attended his live concerts. The guitarist of the American hardcore band Anthrax expressed this rather neatly: "Our album is the menu," he explained. "The concert is the meal." Recovery for the recording industry will require a new strategy and business model, restructuring and reorganization, redeployment of existing talent, and significant recruiting to bring in leaders who can help others move through the paralyzing complexity.

Formula 1 racing, in a similar way to yacht racing, has several parallels to creating alignment in companies. The stakes are high. Teams invest up to $60 million annually to compete. Having a good driver provides an edge, as does having a fast car. But, ultimately, it's teams, not just drivers, that pave the way to victory. Winning requires a team to marshal their resources effectively and execute their unique strategy. Real-time decisions and tactics are made in response to competitors' moves and conditions on race day. Each team's strategy is different. Each team's tactics are tied to its strategy. The timing and speed of tire changes and refueling in the pit can make all the difference. Small errors can have big consequences. Pushing a car too hard can cause a spinout or excessive tire wear. Small misalignments between the pit crew and the driver, and poor execution of tactics, can have a serious impact and even deadly consequences. Seconds, not financial quarters, are the units of performance measurement. And while most of us operate in a somewhat less intense environment, the lessons of alignment, teamwork, and execution are clear.

Whether it's at Apple, IBM, Juicy Couture, PwC, Sterling Commerce, the Martin Agency, or Crown Imports, creating Shockproof alignment requires leaders to challenge the status quo and imagine what *could be* versus what *is*. Too many organizations work on strategy, organization, and talent initiatives in a disjointed, sequential manner. They underestimate the need for connectivity. They focus their attention on organization design one year and talent initiatives the next. What's needed is a more simultaneous approach to calibrating the connections. Sequential efforts take too long and can condemn companies to the *execution treadmill*—lots of effort and sweat equity leading to a sensation of forward movement, but no real progress. Maintaining the muscle memory of Shockproof alignment demands continuous strengthening and toning. Leaders hold the responsibility for building this muscle memory and facilitating alignment. Exactly how do they do it?

# CHAPTER 7

# *Be the Leader You Seek*

Management is doing things right;
leadership is doing the right things.
—Peter F. Drucker

## ONLY LEADERS CAN ALIGN

If aligning strategy, organization, and talent will deliver lasting results, then it makes sense to get on with the job of figuring out how to best link them together, right? Finalize a well-thought-through strategy, design an organization that supports the realization of that strategy, and fill out the structure with the very best people. Done. Finis. Run the credits.

There's only one problem: *Nothing remains the same.*

Changing business conditions creep up unexpectedly, just like new opportunities peek enticingly around the corner. It doesn't matter whether these changes make you sweat or swoon. When change occurs, even the tightest connections among strategy, organization, and talent may bend or break. It becomes the role of leaders to take action to ensure effective recalibration.

When leaders see what has come undone and then act to create or sustain the linkages, Shockproof leadership is in play. Only leaders can align strategy, organization, and talent. Understandably, some leaders end up sitting on the sidelines, feeling overwhelmed by change and complexity, wishing someone else would put the linkages back in place. Fortunately, most leaders recognize the special role they play in influencing and intervening to ensure everyone pulls together toward shared goals and meaningful results.

## POLISH YOUR LENSES

The starting point for leaders to ensure tight connections between strategy, organization, and talent is learning how to use the Shockproof Lenses. Skillfully "worn as a set," these lenses provide a kind of supersensing capability that makes it possible to keep the critical connections among strategy, organization, and talent in place. Think of your experience at the optometrist's office. If your vision is fuzzy, the doctor will move a series of lenses in front of your eyes, one right after another until just the right combination occurs and, bingo, you can now see clearly the letter "E." The Shockproof Lenses work in much the same way. You can start using these five lenses immediately, without resorting to laser surgery. Nothing to misplace; no cleaning solution required!

Shockproof leaders have a keen understanding of the interworkings of each lens. They know when to best use a particular lens to zoom in on an alignment issue, and are bold about bringing some or all of the lenses together to get ahead of potential breeches in the linkages. The Shockproof Lenses allow the "wearer" to apply multiple perspectives and see slight, yet potentially derailing misalignments in the business. In essence, these lenses serve as a kind of "third eye" that points to places where strategy, organization, and talent need tighter connection.

Ironically, though most leaders say they value this kind of consciousness, many "forget" to wear the Shockproof Lenses, or reject their utility altogether. We all know someone who needs to wear eyeglasses but who seems never to have them close at hand. They miss details and nuances that add color and meaning to their lives. Yet many of these people believe they are missing nothing. Nothing important, that is. Others tote Ferragamo spectacles inside Tom Ford glasses cases, but seldom do they see. In other words, they hire advisors, go to conferences, speak the buzzwords, and play the part of consumate leaders. To the untrained eye, they seem to do all the right things, yet very often they fail because they are not truly attending to the things that matter most. Locked in the pattern of seeing what they want to see when they want to—or have to—see it, they may pretend to see at first, only to be outed when they fail to achieve important objectives.

## THE EXTRA POWER OF SHOCKPROOF LENSES

Shockproof Lenses are essential in the quest for real alignment. Simply put, you can't align if you can't see. It is a little like trying to thread a needle while in the dark. It can be done in the dark, but you'll do it with a lot less grief by turning on the light.

Reading this chapter, you will gain a deeper appreciation for each of the Shockproof Lenses and how they are valuable to leaders who wish to improve strategy execution within their organizations. Keep in mind that the lenses are not meant to stand alone. Imagine if you had the ability to see what was going on around you, using the human equivalent of a photographer's panoramic, zoom, and telephoto lenses. You would be able to see better and see more and farther, at the very least. In the same way professional photographers first see the shot they want to take and then use various lenses to take the perfect picture, leaders use the Shockproof Lenses to first discover a new insight and then leverage that insight to help align strategy, organization, and talent.

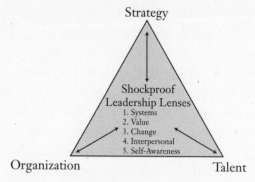

**Figure 7.1    The Shockproof Model**

Figure 7.1, the Shockproof Model, should be familiar to you by now. The new addition is in the center of the triangle where Leadership is composed of the five Shockproof Lenses. These lenses—Systems, Value, Change, Interpersonal, and Self-Awareness—enable Shockproof leaders to maintain the alignment between strategy, organization, and talent.

## THE SYSTEMS LENS: DO YOU SEE WHAT I SEE?

> The *Systems Lens* provides leaders with a wide-angle, pan-oramic perspective that helps them to see the dynamic relationships and connections that exist among business units, functions, processes, technology, and people inside the organization and with external stakeholders (i.e., suppliers, customers, communities, and regulators).

Leaders who are comfortable using the Systems Lens are not surprised by the layers of complexity that exist within their workplaces. The Systems Lens is important to leaders who want to create and maintain a Shockproof organization. It helps them understand what is going on around them. There are fewer surprises when a change in one part of the business causes a ripple effect elsewhere. Rather than being overwhelmed by the dynamic relationships and connections among people and processes, the Shockproof leader who looks through the Systems Lens has a more complete view of the environment. By approaching problem solving with an enterprisewide lens, the leader remains curious as he or she gathers new data and gains new insight. This patience helps the leader sidestep the trap of believing that past practices and conventional ways of operating will always serve the business well in the future.

## Three Focal Points of the Systems Lens

Looking through the Systems Lens, leaders:

1. Seek to understand the relationships that exist among people, processes, and organizations.

   - Value diverse opinions and fresh insight about how things are connected.

   - Pay attention to how assumptions shape perceptions.

2. Look ahead and outside the business; consider not just "what is now," but also "what could be in the future."

   - Monitor industry trends and pending changes that will impact how the business operates.

   - Expect future social, environmental, and political/regulatory shocks to the business and minimize their disruption by preparing accordingly.

3. Know how to zoom in, as well as out, to solve complex problems.

   - Recognize that problems can sometimes be better understood by examining the parts, versus the whole.

- Balance the insight that accompanies zooming out with the clarity that accompanies zooming in.

## A Systems Lens Tale

Remember the example of Larry Clifton (Chapter 5), the former Air Force One officer who achieved a 100 percent reliability rate? Clifton clearly demonstrates the ability to think panoramically and use the Systems Lens to align people, processes, and technologies—not to mention coordinate with high-powered White House officials, and comply with security protocols while never missing a beat. Clifton applied the same systemic thinking to solving talent pipeline and deployment issues at the government contractor CACI. He realized that CACI was leaving dollars on the table by failing to have a 360-degree holistic view of pending contracts, the skill sets of currently deployed contractors, and the likely future talent requirements based on a supply-and-demand approach. He employed a similar level of thoughtful scenario planning that he practiced in his previous role with Air Force One to establish connections across the entire talent management system, which were previously lacking and had an impressive impact on driving costs out of the business.

---

### THE SYSTEMS LENS SHOWCASE

As you read the following business case, focus in particular on how the Shockproof **Systems Lens** was enlisted to help the leader better understand how to create meaningful alignment among strategy, organization, and talent. You will likely see examples of the other Shockproof Lenses within this vignette, as well, but *pay particular attention to the Systems Lens.*

---

## More Than a Pretty Face

The Dermalogica vision has been clear from its founding 20 years ago: To offer a skin care product line free of common irritants, instead loaded with ingredients that improve skin health, and available only from qualified skin therapy professionals who have been trained at the International Dermal Institute (IDI).

As a brand, Dermalogica immediately upset the prevailing paradigm of beauty and glamour by classifying skin care as a health issue, as opposed to a cosmetic concern. Dermalogica also introduced a powerful new element into the brand identity: the specialized expertise of the professional skin therapist. Also, because of company values related to animal testing and intent to keep its corporate identity and jobs in the United States, all its products continue to be manufactured in this country, and the company has never taken part in animal testing. Dermalogica is sold only where treatments can be performed by trained skin therapists. Despite these challenging founder-driven operating principles, Dermalogica has become the number-one choice of skin care professionals worldwide, *prescribed* more often than any other product.

Dermalogica is not owned by a beauty conglomerate, held by a company, or controlled by a group of financiers. The company is driven first and foremost by education and research. The company's founder Jane Wurwand takes pride in being a true pioneer in the industry, growing Dermalogica from a modest storefront in Marina del Rey to the now 145,000-square-foot corporate headquarters in Los Angeles, with locations

*(continued)*

(*continued*)

in close to 50 countries. In 2006, Wurwand recognized that the organization needed to be redesigned to take the company to the "next level" of growth and success. The strategy was to find a President/COO, build and strengthen the management team, and untangle the founders from day-to-day operational issues, so they could focus on their passions—science and education.

When Jerry Wenker was hired as Dermalogica's President/COO, he thought that the skin care phenom would be much less complex to operate than the biopharma world in which he had excelled as a chief marketer. Fortunately, he was a skilled systems thinker, so he was able to appreciate the organization's complexity by zooming out and looking at all its parts and their relationships, before using the insights he had gathered to develop a game plan for the business. "This has been much more complex than I could have imagined," says Wenker. "It took a while to simply take stock of all the moving pieces and their starting and stopping points."[1]

In seeking to understand the relationships that exist among people, processes, and organizations, it became very clear that some new connections had taken hold and that some of the old interdependencies had weakened. For example, the social demographics associated with the company's earliest distribution model shifted and Wenker and his team had to rethink many of the assumptions that had allowed Dermalogica to dominate the market in their earlier years of operation. "Wellness had become ubiquitous, and we needed to work extra hard at differentiating ourselves from everyone else claiming to be in the healthy skin care market," explains

Wenker. Once again, he remained true to his valuing of the Systems Lens in demonstrating his interest in industry trends and pending changes that would likely impact the way the business operated, sooner than later.

Early on, Dermalogica also made a decision to expand into other markets, even before the model was fully proven in the United States. This geographical expansion through rights-controlled markets (United States, Germany, United Kingdom, Australia, Canada) and exclusive distributorships in 50 other markets has been challenging. Over time, the company has been concerned about being too U.S.-centric, rather than operating as a "corporate" entity serving all the distinct markets and businesses. In response, Wenker and his team have had to develop a global/local structure to better align organization design with the businesses and unique markets—a big change for everyone, but one that is proving to be effective. Using the Systems Lens helped Wenker learn about the relationships among various parts of the business, by looking inside and outside, vertically and horizontally. Wenker's ability to see the big picture, without allowing assumptions to hijack planning, contributed to a well-thought-through and supported strategy for improved operational effectiveness.

"Dermalogica is operating in a very different world from our beginnings, and a lot of exciting initiatives have been taken on in the midst of a market [that's] changing due to the increased technology sophistication and mobility of the consumer," shares Wenker. This has added significant complexity to the distribution

*(continued)*

(*continued*)

channels (i.e., emergence of the Internet, home shopping, specialty retailers), versus the simple paradigm of mass (drug store), prestige (department store), and, professional aesthetician of the past. "We have been deliberate in communicating two-way, through the use of strategy forums, round tables, and dialogues, every step of our journey. We all learn together, and we end up making better decisions because we keep discovering new truths," says Wenker, again demonstrating how much he values diversity of opinion and fresh insight, the hallmark of Systems Lens users.

Wenker's leadership acumen, particularly his valuing of the Systems Lens, is one more reason why beauty is more than skin deep at Dermalogica.

## THE VALUE LENS: CUTTING TO THE CORE

The *Value Lens* makes it possible for leaders to see, prioritize, and act on the real, underlying, and primary sources of value; leaders are able to use their understanding of business strategy to defeat the "tyranny of the urgent" and focus instead on those things that are most important to creating long-term value.

When leaders use the Value Lens to interpret what is going on around them, they become highly effective at prioritizing the initiatives and investments that will have the greatest impact on the business. Consider the leaders you know who wish their bottom lines would grow, or that their leadership teams would be more committed and accountable. Maybe you know leaders who wish they could get all the distracting activities and day-to-day firefighting under control, leaving them time to focus on what they know they *should* be doing to create value. Many leaders are passionate; the problem is that good intentions don't automatically translate into results. This is as true in the workplace in the pursuit of profits as it is in life in the pursuit of goals like lower body fat or athletic prowess. Without a clear understanding of what it will take to get to the desired outcome, and without an accompanying realignment of activities and resources to support the goal, most of us don't stand much of a chance of reaching any of our more challenging objectives, at work or at home.

The flip side is that staying focused on those activities that are in alignment with our priorities is the quickest route to the finish line. Leaders may have excellent ideas; team members might talk at length about the possibilities for greater revenue generation; suggestion boxes might overflow with employee hopes and dreams for a better business. But, at the end of the day, if leaders are not harnessing this energy and steering it in the right direction, all too often employees will drift aimlessly, making occasional attempts to hit a moving target, never quite sure of how their day-to-day efforts and contributions count for the business.

## Three Focal Points of the Value Lens

Leaders who see through the Value Lens:

1. Focus attention on the true drivers of value, and revise strategies and tactics as the business evolves.

- Keep the primary value drivers for the business at the core of all activities, constantly reinforcing the linkages between effort and results.

- Discontinue/abandon activities and initiatives that are not directly linked to achieving priorities and creating value.

2. Establish clear connections between day-to-day activities and value creation.

- Clarify what's most important to the business and help people figure out how their day-to-day work contributes to success.

- Recognize when people's efforts are focused on areas of lower priority and ask questions or make suggestions that help them to redirect their contributions.

3. Measure value beyond financial results and consider how a business impacts employees, customers, communities, and the environment.

- Drive financial and operating results while considering social responsibility and the broader environmental context.

- Help people understand the trade-offs inherent in any plan that balances competing priorities.

## A Value Lens Tale

Jim McNulty, the Chicago Mercantile Exchange CEO who presided over the demutalization of the exchange to create a public company, applied his perspective on value to help employees, shareholders, and the Board align around the organization's key priorities. As described in Chapter 4,

McNulty used the Gordon-Shapiro growth model to help this broad group of stakeholders understand value creation using a framework. This was no small task, given the Exchange's long history as a not-for-profit entity. To make "casino owners out of blackjack players," McNulty had to do more than just tell his shareholders what his intentions were; he had to initiate change. In addition to rapidly evolving the organization's vision and strategy, McNulty and his colleagues invested in technology, professionalized staff functions, and introduced new products to grow the value of the business in advance of its public offering. When the CME went public in 2002, its initial public offering raised $166.3 million for shareholders, demonstrating the financial market's support for the newly repositioned entity.

---

## THE VALUE LENS SHOWCASE

As you read the following business case, focus in particular on how the Shockproof **Value Lens** was enlisted to help the leader better understand what needed to be considered to create meaningful alignment among strategy, organization, and talent. You will begin to see examples of the other lenses within this vignette, as well, but train your eyes and your mind to *pay particular attention to the Value Lens.*

### Leadership Goes to the Dogs

When high winds kicked up brush fires in San Diego in October of 2007, Herb Greenberg (a CNBC contributor who appears weekly on programs including

*(continued)*

(*continued*)

*Squawk Box*) and his family headed up Highway 5 and approached a Doubletree Hotel in Anaheim, California, with the hope they could take shelter there. There was only one problem: They were traveling with their West Highland terrier and the hotel's policy was clear: NO PETS ALLOWED.[2]

Surprisingly, the doggy doors opened wide anyway, well ahead of a new pet-friendly policy that was under development at corporate headquarters. So many dogs were welcomed to the hotel that night in fact—and at bargain rates—that regular guests wondered if there was a dog show in town. "It was the right thing to do," General Manager Jeff Protzman told Greenberg at the time.

Protzman's clear understanding of his business's strategic True North made it easy to mobilize his team and get everyone trekking in the same direction. The hotel concierge quickly stocked up on a huge bag of Mother Hubbard's natural canine biscuits; a bellboy was promptly redeployed to act as an on-call dog walker and waste scooper; and the front desk staff deftly remastered the lodging plan for the evening. Relieved pet owners lugged in their dog dishes and leashes, and were checked into one side of the hotel, far from the pet-free guests, wherever possible.

Doubletree's business philosophy is simple and direct: The organization focuses on delivering superior operating profits to its customer—the hotel owners. In return for its management and franchise services, Doubletree is paid a percentage of revenues as a base fee. In addition, Doubletree often receives an incentive fee tied to improvements in hotel operating performance. By consistently creating value for the hotel owner, Doubletree increases its fees and creates value for its stockholders, as well.

The big payoff came when Greenberg wrote in the *Wall Street Journal* weekend investor column about not only his new affinity for Doubletree but also his delight to discover that on the very day he checked out of the Anaheim Doubletree, the Blackstone Group closed on its $26 billion takeover of Hilton (which owns Doubletree). Investors walked away with $47.50 a share, about 600 percent higher than the stock price during Hilton's lows of seven years earlier. Though he didn't hold stock of any kind in any of these transactions, Greenberg pointed out in his column that he was impressed that what he had experienced as a consumer had translated into value for shareholders.

It's easy to see how the Value Lens kept the Anaheim Doubletree's General Manager focused, and his direct reports aligned and clear about what needed to take priority, as business conditions shifted along with the Santa Ana winds.

## THE CHANGE LENS: NOTHING WILL BRING BACK THE HOUR

The *Change Lens* makes it possible for leaders to zoom in and out to see the complexity of change situations, the degree and pace of change that an organization can tolerate, and the most effective methods to align people, communications, and other resources to implement successful change.

Leaders who are facile in the use of the Change Lens recognize that change is about *change* and about *transition*.

What? Sound redundant?

Maybe not.

*Change* is about a move to a new office building or a shift in working hours. It is about the resignation of your mentor, or the mandate to use new technology to perform your work. It is the switch from one group health plan to another, the addition of a major account to your workload, and the new company acquired by your employer.

It does not matter whether you create a change situation, are asked to lead a change situation created by another, or are the one affected by a change situation. Whatever the circumstance, wearing the Change Lens can help you identify the most effective methods to align yourself and others with the desired outcomes.

As a leader, use the Change Lens to help others navigate change in a manner similar to the bullets:[3]

- Develop a clear rationale for the nature and timing of the change.

- Build momentum by sharing background information about what will happen if the change is not realized.

- Mobilize efforts through the work of a guiding coalition.

- Communicate expectations, benefits, and trade-offs, and send aligned messages about the future that is being created.

- Cast a wide net to find the early adopters, and give them room to run; build momentum with quick successes, and integrate new practices where appropriate.

- Combine successes to create a critical mass of support.

Edgar Huber, Juicy Couture's President, helped his business manage change by dividing change into two "buckets." These buckets he called the *mechanics* and *dynamics* of the top team, and he stressed that they were interdependent and equally important to address. "We needed to rebuild and professionalize everything, from design, sales, and marketing to public relations, human resources, and finance."[4] He knew that he could not rebuild the business by focusing only on the mechanics of creating greater clarity around the value drivers and aligning top leaders around priorities, but that he would also need to focus on the dynamics that were connected to the mechanics. For example, he needed his leaders to develop greater self-awareness and to understand how their behavior affected others. He also realized that people needed help with the interpersonal communication skills required to discuss with other work teams what was necessary to effectively collaborate to hit their targets. By paying attention to how his leaders were affected by change (and not just focusing on the change itself), Huber was able to lead Juicy Couture through significant change in a remarkably short period of time.

Successful leaders like Edgar Huber help their teams manage the mechanics and dynamics of change, remembering to create a compelling future state, communicate a believable and understandable rationale for moving on, and offer a workable and comprehensive plan to help people involved in the change get past the real personal costs and losses they are experiencing because of the change.

As priorities change, as new organization structures take shape, and as people use their talents in innovative ways to achieve agreed-upon goals, the change will stir up feelings that will eventually show up at the workplace. Leaders who make time for people, to help them get a handle on what they are feeling, and support them in figuring out what response is right for them, are far more effective in the midst of constant change.

The Change Lens helps leaders manage the change itself and pay attention to the emotional needs associated with it. These skills together help ensure successful execution of strategy. The Change Lens makes it possible to understand simultaneously where the business has been and where it is headed.

## Three Focal Points of the Change Lens

As a result of using this lens, leaders:

1. Identify and communicate the need for change.

   - See the misalignment between the current state and the preferred future.

   - Know how to best communicate the preferred future, the rationale for moving on, and the process to help people let go of the past.

2. Understand how to help people transition through complex change.

   - Understand and address both the mechanics and the dynamics of change.

   - Develop skills that support and enable effective transition.

3. Integrate change management practices into day-to-day workplace activities.

- Recognize how change management practices simplify complexity.

- Utilize change management frameworks, methods, and tools to improve alignment of strategy, organization, and talent.

## *A Change Lens Tale*

Bob Irwin, the former CEO of Sterling Commerce (from Chapter 3) clearly understood the dynamics of change and why leaders in his company needed to use the Change Lens effectively. As Irwin related, "It took [us] almost 18 months to get everybody to truly believe [in the strategy]."[5] His "ladder of human dynamics" framework helped others develop the patience to see change through to successful completion. The seven key steps are to: (1) hear (sound), (2) listen (meaning), (3) understand (internalize), (4) believe (accept), (5) commit (enroll), (6) engage (act), and—voilà!—(7) *change*. Irwin demonstrates a clear awareness that change is hard; also that it is absolutely essential that leaders learn how to stick with it, until people are securely on board.

---

### THE CHANGE LENS SHOWCASE

As you read the following business case, focus in particular on how the Shockproof **Change Lens** was enlisted to help the leader better understand what needed to be

(*continued*)

*(continued)*

considered to create meaningful alignment among strategy, organization, and talent. You will likely see examples of the other Shockproof Lenses within this vignette, as well, but train your eyes and your mind to *pay particular attention to the Change Lens*.

## Compound Returns

When pharmaceuticals giant Pfizer began to experience all the indicators of a business in decline in the late 1990s and early 2000s, new leadership at the top set out to tackle the problem. After setting profitability records within the industry in the early to mid-1990s, the business invested heavily in its own R&D. However, a number of complex business conditions began to dovetail, including patent expiry, increasingly complex deals between biotech and big pharma, health care regulation, and insurance provider formularies. As Pfizer grew, functional business units became more and more parochial, and trust began to erode among key business leaders as a battle for succession to the CEO played out.

The internal new-product pipeline was soon deemed grossly inadequate. Lisa Ricciardi, a whiz-kid marketer who had been instrumental in successful blockbuster drug launches such as Lipitor and Zithromax, was called upon to head up Licensing, an organization that primarily facilitated the evaluation of very early-stage deal opportunities. She soon learned that the Licensing and Development Group (L&D) turned out to be a "wait station" for executives who didn't fit the usual commercial drug franchise model. They sat in Licensing and waited—until they retired. Traditionally, the heavy hitters at Pfizer were the highly analytical financial gurus who performed due diligence on deal opportunities, and the equally clout-carrying technical specialists who weighed in on the science behind the compounds. The Licensing organization was the bridge between these two entities, acting as highly paid moderators, rather than serving as Licensing professionals.

Throughout the Licensing organization, both Ricciardi's team and the larger matrix of stakeholders began to become more clear about the value Licensing could play in evaluating opportunities against an agreed set of standards. Ricciardi knew how to lead change, so she focused on how to best communicate the preferred future and facilitated a discussion with the larger licensing system to help them get aligned.

A natural Shockproof thinker, Ricciardi decided to "pull everyone together to fully and openly discuss where we were headed and what we had all been asked to do."[6] Along the way, she tapped into a wide array of change management frameworks, methods, and tools to improve her ability to align strategy, organization, and talent.

Her direct reports spent many weeks openly discussing what was changing and why. The performance bar was raised immediately for all of them, and not many made it through the first year. As the new change took hold, Ricciardi began to influence the makeup of Licensing's larger structure. "This was no easy task, and we never got it 100 percent right," she elaborates, "but we were eventually able to reach unthinkable financial targets that would have been all but impossible to achieve had we not focused on simply aligning the key

(*continued*)

(*continued*)

players. . . ." These simple practices are a sign of the Change Lens in action and Ricciardi's commitment to helping others adapt.

Pfizer's U.S. President at that time remarked that Ricciardi's leadership had led to three highly disparate divisions working together successfully to do important licensing deals better, smarter, and faster than their competitors. In fact, between 1998 and 2004, the Licensing organization was able to acquire compounds that improved the pipeline by almost $8 billion.

At one point, Ricciardi brought together the key leaders from Finance, R&D, Commercial, and Licensing to create a new organization design that clarified primary and secondary decision responsibilities. The process was grueling and countercultural in its focus on collaboration, "but it was the beginning of the transformation in the way we did business," she said, and over time the lines between interdependent work groups were less bold.

Once the right team was in place and its members began performing together, Ricciardi and her direct reports began to lead improvements in operating practices, processes, and even team norms. "We worked on building our team so we could cascade improvements throughout the licensing matrix," Ricciardi explained. "We developed leaders so they would have better listening and negotiating skills. Everyone became crystal clear about their accountabilities and their strengths and weaknesses. As organization effectiveness needs emerged, I assigned members of my team to work with corporate staff and outside consultants to determine what should happen next."

The way we see it, Ricciardi's change acumen ultimately created a way for people to contribute to *making something extraordinary happen*—together. The array of compounds needed to supplement the eroding portfolios of Pfizer's major disease system franchises was formidable, and Ricciardi*'s* team paved the way to success.

## THE INTERPERSONAL LENS: ADVOCACY AND INQUIRY

The *Interpersonal Lens* makes it possible for leaders to see how to best understand, empathize, and connect with people to forge relationships that combine trust, mutual respect, and learning.

Interpersonal communication is the exchange that takes place between people who are in some way "connected." Through words, tone of voice, and nonverbal behaviors of others, leaders can learn how to connect in full with the messages sent by others, and decode those messages, down to the nuance. By looking through the Interpersonal Lens, leaders see things that are often missed by those who are disinclined to develop a real connection with other people. Effective use of the Interpersonal Lens gives leaders the space to test their understanding of both the verbal and written messages they receive. By tuning into the cues and clues sent by other people, the leader gains insights into who they are and what they need. This information helps leaders adapt their leadership styles and communication methods to better fit with the preferences of others, which ultimately helps them relate better to employees. A primary tool associated with the Interpersonal Lens is *appreciative inquiry*, a sophisticated listening and questioning practice of remaining "in the moment" with the communicator to gather accurate information and increase new understanding.

The Interpersonal Lens makes it possible to gain an understanding of what people need to be successful, why people do not always approach problem solving in the same way, and how to adapt one's own repertoire of skills to build rapport and trust. Leaders who value the Interpersonal Lens will demonstrate the ability to listen actively, to check assumptions, and to spend time getting to know people beyond who they are in their work roles. When using the Interpersonal Lens, leaders learn how to critically observe and engage, in an attempt to find more value and discover points of connection. They demonstrate patience, respect, and curiosity in their relationships with others.

## Three Focal Points of the Interpersonal Lens

When leaders look through this lens they:

1. Appreciate individuals of diverse backgrounds, experiences, and approaches.

   - Invite people to participate in dialogues and facilitate the discussion of conflicting points of view.

   - Adapt to individual preferences and know how to leverage the strengths of others.

2. Encourage the balanced use of inquiry and advocacy.

   - Model concise, clear, and compelling advocacy.

- Practice active listening to guard against faulty assumptions and inferences.

3. Inspire trust and respect through the effective use of multiple communication methods.

   - Move from one communication channel to another with ease, such as one-to-one, group, and written communications.

   - Practice openness, soliciting and sharing feedback to build trust and respect.

## An Interpersonal Lens Tale

Harry Kraemer, the former CEO of global health care giant Baxter (from Chapter 3) subscribes to the view that leaders need to apply the Interpersonal Lens to forge the types of trusting relationships that make possible frank, open, and honest dialogue and discussion. He believes that getting the right level of engagement and reflection from leaders involved in strategy development, for example, is essential. This would include openness, soliciting feedback, and sharing perspectives. Kraemer asserts that open debate and dialog between leaders with different points of view will enable them as a group to get to the right answer. Kraemer recognizes that relationships that support open, honest dialogue don't happen overnight. "To be trusted, one needs to prove oneself trustworthy and of high integrity; and it takes time," he says.[7] Kraemer believes that the payoff from investing in these relationships is that "when a difficult challenge occurs and tough decisions need to be made, leaders will help each other do the right thing and make the right decisions," for the business, its customers, employees, and shareholders.

## THE INTERPERSONAL LENS SHOWCASE

As you read the following business case, focus in particular on how the Shockproof **Interpersonal Lens** was enlisted to help the leader create meaningful alignment among strategy, organization, and talent. You will likely see examples of the other Shockproof Lenses within this vignette, as well, but *pay particular attention to the Interpersonal Lens*.

### More Than Just a Banner Year

Michael Fleming, EdD, recently served in the top Human Resources job at Banner Health, one of the largest nonprofit hospital systems in the United States. Dr. Fleming tells us, "Our hospital leaders have been charged with doing more with less. People who once clamored to work in a healing profession have become increasingly disillusioned by changes within health care."[8] Political uncertainties, staggering increases in individual workload and span of control, and the need to manage complex dynamics associated with government regulations, outside clinics, revenue recovery, and patient rights have made employment within hospitals less attractive, in general, and less financially rewarding, specifically. Fleming talks about the intention and effort expended to help employees stay focused on what matters. "They continually wonder: Will we have jobs? Will we ever make any more money? Will we be able to do good work? What's coming next?"

In 2005 Banner leadership realized that being the smartest clinically and technically wasn't going to secure their place as a top-performing provider. As Fleming tells it, "The reality was that without equal strength on the interpersonal side 'we simply couldn't make it.' Once we understood and accepted that relationships were the platform upon which the entire business model rested, working with leaders to become experts in communication became an imperative. Listening to patients, to direct reports, and to each other; learning how to see and manage conflict; and acting with courage to change a strongly held point of view rose to the top of our strategic priorities."

Banner leaders came to understand that a major driver of value for the Banner hospital system is the creation of "a kind of talent intimacy." By this I mean that those who provide contributions for us need to know that we will make genuine attempts to ensure that they will not be better heard, valued, or treated anywhere else than they will with us here at Banner," says Fleming.

"We promote open and candid dialogues," Fleming adds, "and equip managers with the information they need . . . to ensure [that] the people they lead feel [as if they're] in on things, know how the work they do makes a difference, every day, and that they are supported in innovative work arrangements so they can take care of their families and improve themselves."

To support advancement of the interpersonal theme as a business strategy, Banner launched "Leadership Matters," a series of integrated changes in its performance management model, vastly improving both the accuracy and granularity of patient feedback, upgrading an emphasis on and precision around effective talent management, and specifically redefining systems of evaluation, reward, and recognition. This commitment to the interpersonal dimension was anchored by a 36-hour

*(continued)*

*(continued)*

leadership development initiative. Woven throughout all aspects of this imperative was the expectation that a profound focus on the interpersonal communication dimension—especially, clear, quality "sending" and "receiving"—would be the cornerstone of their long-term success as an organization.

"Overall," Fleming continued, "we developed people to be able to give and receive feedback—crisp, clear, and quick. Banner's business moves too fast; the stakes are too high. Leaders have to be open to what their employees think and need, and offer honest responses." Says Fleming, "Banner regularly invites employees and patients to participate in dialogues without concern about conflicting points of view."

The results have been impressive. Patient satisfaction scores are rapidly reaching the top decile, employee retention is at an all-time high, and increasingly, Banner is perceived nationally as "a place where your voice is heard" and "your contribution to its great mission is acknowledged and appreciated—not once a year, but every day." This interpersonal bond of dignity, respect, and clear communication calls patients, families, and staff to adapt and respond with strength and loyalty to the massive uncertainty health care faces. Between 2008 and 2009 Banner experienced 8.8 percent revenue growth with operating margins more than doubling to 7.4 percent.[9]

Given these foundations and level of alignment and commitment, it looks as if the high-performance flag will keep waving at Banner for a very long time, easily seen by its growing cadre of leaders, skillful in the use of the Interpersonal Lens.

# THE SELF-AWARENESS LENS: MIRROR, MIRROR ON THE WALL

The *Self-Awareness Lens* makes it possible for leaders to look in the mirror to gain insight into self, including strengths and weaknesses, personality, style preferences, interests, and values.

The Self-Awareness Lens is the one most often lost or buried in the bottom of the leader's bag. Leaders see the word *self-awareness* and they back off as though the word itself might cause them to lose their ability to control the world around them. Yet self-aware leaders hold the keys to the castle. Leaders from CEO Glenn Senk of Urban Outfitters to CEO Alysa Miller of Public Radio International advised University of Chicago Booth School of Business MBA students to "become self-aware by seeking as many varied experiences as possible, developing emotional intelligence and using good listening skills,"[10] as doing so provides a competitive edge. Leaders who are self-aware know what they treasure and hold dear; they understand how to pave the right path by tapping into their wisdom; and they are fearless.

On the other hand, the experience of getting to really know oneself, and one's personal power, can be unsettling. When leaders focus attention on themselves, they may end up evaluating and comparing their current behaviors to their internal standards and values—or, worse, to those of others. They become self-conscious and may end up overcriticizing themselves and losing confidence.

Self-awareness does not happen overnight, and it isn't a skill that can be taught in a classroom or acquired simply by reading a book. Self-awareness develops over time, through a willingness to receive feedback, reflect on the perspectives of others, consider new ways of being or acting, practice new behaviors, and incorporate into one's own leadership style fresh ways of "showing up." In this regard, self-awareness begins with a decision to see oneself in a new light, perhaps one that is more or less attractive than the one a person has been using for years. However tough it may be for people to look into themselves and see who they really are, other people are more likely to want to follow the leader who has real self-insight and understanding.

Looking through the Self-Awareness Lens makes it possible to see from the outside as well as from the inside. Such a leader will pay attention to inner thoughts, physical well-being, spiritual needs, intimacies, and finding and acting on a sense of purpose in living his or her life. Leaders who value the Self-Awareness Lens will demonstrate the ability to be still, reflect before responding, admit mistakes, modify patterns of behavior, and seek ongoing opportunities for learning through feedback and new experiences. Instead of trying to become what he or she is not, the self-aware leader grows comfortable becoming more of who he or she really is, including all the flaws and idiosyncrasies that are part of being human. Self-awareness helps leaders work up an appetite for new insights; they get comfortable with going deep into conversation with others, becoming transparent, and erring on the side of openness. Self-aware leaders have an appreciation for the role leadership plays in all facets of their lives, and they seek to integrate and align their values with their behaviors.

## Three Focal Points of the Self-Awareness Lens

Looking through the Self-Awareness Lens, leaders:

1. Commit to growing and learning every day.

   - Admit mistakes.

   - Show humility, yet remain determined.

2. Practice "the art of going deep," to gain new insight and understanding.

   - Engage in self-reflective activities that make personal space for stillness and contemplation.

   - Have the strength to stay with especially challenging or difficult circumstances until they are resolved.

3. Remain authentic, yet other-centered.

   - Treat all people with genuine respect (as opposed to just going through the motions).

   - Understand the importance of aligning intentions with word, tone, and nonverbal behavior.

## A Self-Awareness Lens Tale

Looking back on the most challenging aspects of leading change at Crown Imports LLC, Bill Hackett (from Chapter 6), a president who likes to take a hands-on approach to the business said, "I stayed out of the way and let Bruce [Jacobson, EVP of Sales] and his team do the work."[11] Hackett has a high level of self-awareness, and that comes shining through in his ability to see that he does not have to be at the center of an alignment effort. Neither does he feel compelled to have all of the answers himself, nor does he feel the need to overly direct others. He invests his time developing and challenging people in key roles and relies on them to deliver results. "Knowing that the process was outside of my direct purview was painful, but I put a lot of faith in Bruce's commitment and passion to making it work." The self-aware leader recognizes that others have needs that may be more important than his or her own, such as the need to lead a major initiative and not have their boss overseeing every move. Hackett was mindful of his tendency to want to "get into the weeds and do the work," but understood that this would not lead to the best result for Crown Imports. This self-awareness was good for Hackett and good for the business.

## THE SELF-AWARENESS LENS SHOWCASE

As you read the following business case, focus in particular on how the Shockproof **Self-Awareness Lens** was enlisted to help the leader better understand what needed to be considered to create meaningful alignment among strategy, organization, and talent. You will likely see examples of the other Shockproof Lenses within this vignette, as well, but *pay particular attention to the Self-Awareness Lens.*

### Growing Up Shockproof

"We have a very disruptive technology at Memjet,"[12] CEO Len Lauer says. "We hold 3,000 approved patents and are a well-invested start-up, with all the right things in place to grow to a billion and be in excellent shape for an IPO." But Lauer also knows that despite the power of a next-generation printer technology, he and his leadership team are the key to driving the business to the successful execution of a very clear strategy.

"Good leaders know how to integrate external drivers against internal capabilities. I value this and expect my leaders to do the same. I coach them and give them feedback if they get off track. I set very clear expectations." Lauer's expectations are, of course, focused on strategic priorities, operating goals, and metrics. He is equally interested in every one of his direct reports putting the team first by resolving issues related to collaboration and committment. There is little room for self centeredness or inflated egos. Lauer believes in knowing himself and his strengths and weaknesses, and expects the same of those on his team. He also stresses the value of having an executive coach, since his work with coaches helped him become more mindful of his leadership behaviors and the value of being regarded as vulnerable and human. He explains: "Top leaders have had much experience being told that they have brought about good business results; and they are generally very bright. This is a dangerous combination because such a leader usually gets things very quickly, and can seem arrogant, impatient, and unapproachable." Lauer say the solution is to "humanize oneself, so others will see you as a real person. Talk about mistakes you have made from time to time when with others. Share how you learned from those mistakes."

Lauer also was open about the value of asking questions of people throughout the organization, and listening patiently to their answers about what they do outside of their business-related roles, and who they are as individuals. He learned through his own process of self-reflection, and through feedback, that others sometimes saw him as invulnerable, and this made it tougher for people to both relate to him and support him. "People were looking for me to make a mistake."

Real leaders are leading and getting things done long before they have any kind of positional power on an organization chart. They know themselves and they become the best they can be. They focus on becoming "good guys" (both men and women)—far from perfect, but the best they can be. The idea is to know your strengths and keep getting better at those. Surround yourself with people who can make up for the rest. Better to fess up about both strengths and weaknesses, and start leading.

## ARE YOU BEGINNING TO SEE THINGS MORE CLEARLY?

If you think it through, there is nothing singularly daunting about any one of the preceding leadership studies. In fact, you can probably see parts of yourself or other leaders you admire in the examples of these Shockproof leaders. We all have many of these abilities, and they show up in our work every day. Yet in these portrayals, laid out one after another, we can recognize an exceptional sort of leadership awareness and intention that permeates them all. These leaders seem to indeed be operating using special lenses—lenses that help them navigate by looking out, looking in, looking over, and looking under, seemingly without effort and always without missing a beat.

Are you now feeling ready to use the Shockproof Lenses yourself? Keep in mind there is only one rule: Wear them! Next let's see what happens when a leader actually demonstrates that he sees value in using all the lenses all the time. It is a blazing-hot story. And like our other examples, it involves a real leader focusing on delivering real results.

## SWEATING THE WAY UP THE PERFORMANCE CHART

The Warnaco Group, Inc., headquartered in New York, is a leading apparel company engaged in the business of designing, sourcing, marketing, and selling intimate apparel, menswear, jeanswear, swimwear, men's and women's sportswear, and accessories. One licensed brand is Calvin Klein Jeans (CKJ). CKJ is led by President David Cunningham. He has held this position since the onset of a very popular series of ads featuring Eva Mendes, who is seemingly stuck to a billboard by the sweat layering up around the waistband of her Calvin Klein Jeans.

No neophyte to the world of lifestyle brands like CKJ, Cunningham had previously and successfully served as President of Chaps (also a Warnaco holding). When he was President of Chaps, Cunningham found it necessary to pull apart the business and put it back together in a new way, to get the results he was asked to achieve. In particular, thanks to his **Value Lens**, he led an effort to eliminate practices that did not contribute to achieving priorities and adding value. As he considered his transition to Calvin Klein Jeans, Cunningham initially believed he'd need only tweezers, versus the usual scalpel to clean things up at CKJ.[13] After all, CKJ was a very strong global brand, perceived by many as an exceptionally well-run business. Since the introduction of the original Calvin Klein Jean in 1978, when Brooke Shields stared at the camera and purred, "Nothing gets between me and my Calvin Kleins—and I mean nothing," Calvin Klein Jeans has always been a driving force in the fashion world.

However, after several months spent immersing himself in the business, Cunningham discovered he would have to tailor the CKJ organization by tightening up the operating model a bit. Cunningham's **Systems Lens** pointed him in the direction of diving in deeper, to understand some of the key parts of the overall organization, before taking action. He suspended judgment and used multiple perspectives and sources of performance data to develop a new strategic plan. The lines of demarcation were clear as to where Warnaco, the operator, and Calvin Klein, the brand owner, were concerned. His greater challenge was closer to home—his team. Cunningham discovered that the business was far more fragmented than he had anticipated, riddled with the special interests of the various company sites and maimed by perceptions of functional hierarchy and self-importance. Adding to the disfigurement was the complexity of the men and women's collections. Fortunately, as a wearer of the **Systems Lens**, Cunningham was able to tap into the insight that comes from divergent points of view. He helped others find common ground, and with that clarity, everyone stayed focused on new priorities.

The value of this clarity was paramount when Cunningham's **Interpersonal Lens** focused him on raising the bar on the integrated and collaborated efforts of the CKJ Global Brand team. Early on, the team was charged with reaching agreement about the key drivers of value creation; then they set to work together to prioritize actions and integrate plans. By decreasing the size of the team and making their shared goals absolutely clear, the Global Brand team members were able to concentrate together on a specific subset of their ever-growing priorities. They found that the time they spent together, shielded from interruptions and forced to build deeper relationships, helped accelerate their alignment around their charter and increased their ability to solve problems after they returned to their respective offices in Europe and Asia.

Beyond the global brand's charge, Cunningham continued to drill down, focusing on the key driver of retail sales: planning. His **Value Lens** kept zeroing in on the need to establish clear connections between day-to-day activities and value creation. Retail plans became critical maps for the development of solid merchandizing plans for the future season. These improvements in planning exponentially helped the stores know exactly which products they should carry, and also gave the designers more direction about what to create, without interfering with their creative process. For example, by understanding price points, the designers avoided falling in love with a fabric that wouldn't fit the plan. Thus, no store would be stuck with a great product languishing on reduction racks in the basement inventory simply because the garment's price point didn't meet that particular store's circumstances. To get these handoffs to work, people had to begin by wanting to work together; then they had to have the skills to collaborate and see the big picture.

Beyond the retail and merchandizing plans, a second key part of planning was financial forecasting. The kind of data needed was growing in complexity, and the necessary analysis was becoming more sophisticated. Cunningham soon realized that CKJ needed planners to be singularly focused on either retail responsibilities or financial planning. In the past, planners were hired to perform both jobs and were forced to split their time between the demands of retail and financial planning. However, most planners were more skillful at one kind of planning, not both; they demanded different competencies. It became clear to Cunningham that redesigning the planner job was essential so that people who were really good at retail planning could focus on just retail across all the divisions, and people who were really good at financial planning could focus on financial forecasting across all the divisions. Cunningham continued the talent readjustments in both design and graphics. To help get the process calendars aligned for men's and women's seasonal collections, he also promoted one person to head up both groups.

Cunningham made these changes while also managing the expectation of the parent company to change out talent, versus redesign the job. By understanding how to lead planned change and integrate change management into the way he worked with the business heads day to day, Cunningham was skillful in not only redesigning jobs but also tweaking the structure and engaging interdependent functional leads in the improvement of the overall planning process. As business results began to improve, the skeptics backed down and "are quiet" for now. For Cunningham, looking through the **Change Lens**, this was success: "I don't need them to love everything I do. I just need them to let me get the needed change in place so the results can take hold."

Turning back to his own team, Cunningham stated that, "At times, I had to lead through some natural resistance to change. But I have learned to be patient. Once the right people and processes are in place, I know that eventually [they] will get comfortable with change that helps us all to succeed." He learned to be patient and unflappable. As long as he remained open and clear about what they are moving toward, and why they needed to go there, helped them see that others were also moving in the same direction, and kept refocusing them on their new responsibilities, reminded them that they are being asked to be a part of the change because of capabilities they possess, and that are needed, and demonstrated his own deep commitment to the change, he knew they would all eventually reach their shared goals, every one of them. No small feat, but it's fascinating that Cunningham was clear about what it takes to help people move through change, without losing patience or momentum as they passed through various stages of resistance before finally becoming comfortable with the adjustments he made to the way that they worked.

Cunningham also pays special attention to leaders when they are first in their new roles, whether they are "outside" new hires, or inside placements. "I touch base with them personally at the 30-, 60-, and 90-day marks, to help them sort out the ebb and flow of their new roles. I don't let this slide. I know that the leader may well fail if he or she isn't helped to align and integrate." Too often, Cunningham says, he has seen top leaders relegate this responsibility elsewhere in the business. He believes it is critical to keeping everyone on the same page.

Cunningham demonstrated his use of the **Self-Awareness Lens** when he shared his beliefs about what has helped him navigate through a lengthy or complex transition. "I have become more self-aware, more self-scrutinizing over the years. I know I can bulldoze through with my ideas. Yet by staying true to my intentions, in what I say [and] how I say it, and 'show up,' people eventually buy in, understand, and feel supported in their slow leap from the old to the new. I will end up trusting those same folks to keep things moving in the right direction, even when I have turned to focus on the next thing that needs my attention."

Throughout the reformation of his team, Cunningham's actions were emblematic of a Shockproof leader mentality. This claim is reinforced by the results of a 2009 Axiom Consulting Group strategy execution study in which Warnaco was ranked number one in the top performing quartile of companies.[14] These companies, according to the study, "were more likely to have leaders and professionals throughout the organization recognize the enterprisewide implications of their actions" and "apply an enterprisewide perspective to local business problems." Cunningham's commitment to Shockproofing, and his success in using the Shockproof Lenses to create greater alignment, are testimonials to the extra value derived from the use of the lenses. Warnaco's net income a year after Cunningham's promotion—and smack-dab in the middle of the worst of the 2008–2009 recession—rose 28 percent, helped by gains in its Calvin Klein and Chaps businesses. (Don't forget, Cunningham ran Chaps before taking over at Calvin Klein.) As a result of those performance improvements, Warnaco reported that its net income rose to $48 million, or $1.02 per share, from $37.6 million, or 81 cents per share. Some well-deserved wiping of the sweat from David Cunningham's brow is expected.

## THE SHOCKPROOF LEADER DIFFERENCE

It is fairly easy to identify leaders who are working to Shockproof their businesses. When talking with others in the organization, the Shockproof leader finds natural and effective ways to bring the conversation back to drivers of value for the business, and will explore what is helping or blocking others in their efforts to achieve shared goals. They have the courage to ask powerful questions in a straightforward yet respectful way, and seem to know exactly which questions to ask to keep people focused on doing the right things. When too many people are battling it out for airtime, these leaders know how to slow things down and help people really listen to one another, rather than shutting down potentially meaningful communication. When Shockproof leaders themselves come up short in some way, they talk openly with others about what they had trouble achieving in the past, and they ask for ideas about how they might do better the next time. They balance the art of simplifying complexity with the importance of letting individuals wrestle with ambiguity and paradox. Shockproof leaders demonstrate the uncanny ability to *see more and see better*, so it really does seem that they wear special lenses that help them navigate their businesses around hairpin turns and over long stretches of open road.

# CHAPTER 8

# *Pass the Salt*

The difference between getting somewhere and nowhere is the courage to make an early start.
—Charles Schwab

I t's been a week since you downloaded and read your first article about Shockproof businesses.

This interest in high-performing companies was no idle Sunday afternoon surf of the Web. Your exploration was the response to the enthusiastic fallout of your CEO's inspirational and insistent charge to you and your teammates at a company townhall last week. She was thorough and crystal clear about last year's business performance, and announced that job number one for the executive team was to work together to achieve an aggressive set of revenue growth and profitability goals. From the outset, those goals seemed insurmountable and exhausting, and she acknowledged they would be tough to reach:

> Reaching these objectives will be difficult, especially in light of the increasingly challenging macroeconomic, social, environmental, and regulatory challenges facing our industry. However, you are a talented group of leaders; each of you demonstrates your commitment every day to overcoming significant obstacles and hurdles.

She added that she was confident you would, together, figure out how to crack the code on your company's flat performance, and reminded you that the complexity in your operating environment was likely to increase. You found it refreshing to hear her straight-talking reflections on the business, the road ahead, and what it would take to achieve these challenging goals.

> I encourage each one of you to come back to our next meeting, a few short months from now, prepared to challenge each other and yourselves concerning how we do things today. Be ready to stretch your thinking on what's possible, and be willing to not only share your ideas but to really listen to the ideas of others. As far as I'm concerned, everything is on the table for consideration.

At the end of the CEO's presentation, you were selected to gather input from your colleagues to help shape the agenda for the next offsite, three months later. This assignment led you to pay close attention to what other companies had done to manage through complexity and reach their growth and performance goals. Your iPad has been on fire all week with all the information you're pulling from the Internet.

The mother lode has turned out to be the seminal work itself, the simple story of how to hardwire one's business for lasting success. Your scan of the Internet to find out more about those businesses that have been dubbed Shockproof keeps bringing up the same results: agile, adaptable, able to withstand shocks, and capitalizes on opportunities.

Based on what you have been learning, you are convinced that the goals laid out by your CEO will not be achievable if the way people problem solve today doesn't change. You and your peers tackle problems in silos, and work independently to execute strategy, improve work processes, and manage people. You now know that an integrated and aligned approach is much more likely to work.

The implications are clear. Your executive team peers will need to fundamentally change the way they approach making improvements in operational effectiveness, and how people are managed and led. It seems that there has always been a preference to tackle issues sequentially. You know from discussions with your peers that this preference comes from a concern about losing control over one's own area of responsibility, or having to work with others who do not share the same priorities or problem-solving approach. Achieving the task ahead will require a more dynamic approach than is the norm, but how to get there?

Throughout the week you have been scribbling in your iPad notes pages as you came across studies, articles, and books that seemed to have some relevance to the notion of Shockproof versus shockprone. Three of these questions move to the top of your list.

1. Is the Shockproof Model right for our business?

2. If so, how can I engage the rest of the executive team to participate in Shockproofing our business?

3. Am I ready and willing to use the Shockproof Lenses to do my part to help align strategy, organization, and talent?

You know that the answers to the first two questions will become clearer after you meet with each of your peers, which you plan to do over the next few weeks. You enlarge question 1 on your iPad screen and ponder possibilities. You are excited about what Shockproofing can do for your business, but you also know you are just one of eight members of the executive team, so you want to be careful not to get too far ahead of the others. After all, the company has been through a lot of turmoil recently and everyone, including you, has little appetite for anything that might feel too big to digest.

Initially, you were concerned that introducing the Shockproof Model would cause leaders to feel overwhelmed. But as
you tap your finger on the first question, the notes you wrote
about *readiness* and how to introduce the approach pop up:

- One blogger who adopted Shockproof thinking
  commented that the best way to introduce the
  approach is to get the right people in the room and start
  by asking simple, focused questions. He reported
  that asking questions about what's broken in the
  business is a good first step. Additionally, asking
  leaders to think about how they lead today and how
  they can lead more effectively using the Shockproof
  Lenses helped stimulate the impetus for change.

- A business leader reports that the approach gained
  traction once his peers realized that it's not a flavor-
  of-the-month idea. It simply represents a more integrated perspective on how leaders can align strategy,
  organization, and talent to deliver results. No "special sauce" required.

- A mid-level manager at a software company said that she
  introduced the Shockproof Model in her department to
  get priorities, work processes, and people in synch.

Good, you think to yourself. The notes are an important
reminder. The approach can start with C-suite leaders, but it
doesn't have to. You like that this work can start anywhere in the
company—wherever there is genuine readiness. There is one
more note under question 1 so you grab it and expand the text:

- Since the Shockproof approach is focused on unlocking value, would the business benefit from a structured
  discussion on the topic?

The suggested exercise that you read about and jotted down earlier seems straightforward: If every key leader in your business were asked *at this moment* to write their own answers to the following questions on large index cards, how many of the answers would be the same?

1. How do we define value?
2. What organizational capabilities and activities drive the most value?
3. To what extent are our collective priorities consistent and focused on what drives the greatest value?

These simple questions are provocative. You're pretty sure that they will promote good dialogue and discussion. It feels like it's been a long time since leaders took a step back and engaged in this level of clarification about what drives value and whether or not the business is focused on the right priorities. You start to feel more confident that this type of thinking will be helpful at the offsite. It's seems like exactly what's needed to help the executive team respond to your CEO's challenge. You will use the one-on-one meetings with the other leaders to see if they agree that this will be a good discussion topic at the offsite.

You open your calendar and the calendars of your six peers and your manager, the CEO. With a couple of touches on the calendar icon, all eight calendars pop up in front of you. You hit the "sync week" function and plug in your scheduling criteria. Bingo. In seconds you have a list of dates and times that will work for you and each executive.

With a voice command you load in a short audio message that will be delivered when your invitation is received:

*"I'd like to get your thoughts about how to more aggressively grow the business. Your insight will help me construct an agenda for the next executive meeting, so I have set up an hour for us to talk. Thanks!"*

Next, you jot down a number of questions for your one-on-one meetings, surprised by how differently you are analyzing the business. It isn't completely natural for you to think this way, and you are a little bit clumsy at first, but at least you are keeping alignment and execution front and center. You come up with the following questions for the interviews:

### Strategy

1. Do you believe that everyone, from the boardroom to our people on the frontline, would describe our strategy the same way?

2. What do you see as our three to five most strategic priorities, and do you think everyone on the executive team would agree?

3. What is getting attention right now that is not in line with our priorities; what isn't getting priority right now and needs more of our attention and focus?

### Organization

1. Does our current organization design support effective execution of our strategy and priorities?

2. Do we have the right workflows and work processes in place?

3. Is everyone clear about roles, responsibilities, decision rights, and the performance metrics that link their contributions to our strategy?

### Talent

1. Do our people have the skills, knowledge, and abilities to do the work that needs to be performed to execute the strategy?

2. From your perspective, in which areas do you see the greatest talent gaps?

3. How effective are we at acquiring, developing, deploying, rewarding, and keeping the right people?

During your preparation, you make another list of questions, using the Shockproof Lenses as a guide (see Figure 8.1). You know these questions will help you and the other executives gain new understanding about how to better align strategy, organization, and talent, so you capture these questions in a pull-down menu on your iPad. You label the menu "Shockproof Lens Questions" so you can easily find them later during the interview. You will use them to draw out insights during each interview about how leaders are thinking about the business.

You run these questions past a few of your colleagues and the CEO, and after getting the green light, move forward the next day with the interviews. A few weeks later, you have completed all seven interviews. Some of the team members have been part of the business since it was founded 22 years ago. Others have been on board just a few years. While completing the interviews, you were asked to add to the mix a number of additional stakeholder interviews. They include the owner of a lean manufacturing initiative that has been in place for five years; the head of Human Resources, who is not a member of the executive team; a few board members; and a former CEO, who retired two years ago. Their perspectives add richness to the data.

**Systems Lens:**

• What external trends (industry, social, technological, political) should we pay
  attention to?
• Who are the key stakeholders in our business, including customers, external partners,
  and suppliers that have the greatest influence on our ability to achieve our objectives?
• Who are the leaders in our business that always seem to get things done—and deliver
  results even when the rest of us are struggling?
• Do you see any misalignments between our strategy, organization, technology
  infrastructure, and talent?

**Value Lens:**

• Of the activities and initiatives that we are focused on today, which ones are clearly
  linked to the key sources of value for our business?
• Which initiatives distract us from our top priorities and dilute value?
• Do you think people know how their work and daily activities create value?
• Are there other factors that influence value creation that we should consider more
  closely such as practices that help protect the environment or the well-being of people
  inside and outside the business in the communities we serve?

**Change Lens:**

• Do we appreciate the complexity, degree, and pace of change that the organization
  can tolerate?
• Which initiatives are we struggling to implement effectively? And, what can we
  do to better manage the changes?
• How can we better align our communication practices with the way we manage change?
• What beliefs do we have about how change should be managed (e.g., *get on with it, people
  can't change, change is a bad thing*) that may need to be further explored or challenged?

**Interpersonal Lens:**

• Is there anything about the way we work with each other that may be getting in the
  way of people performing at their best?
• What relationship skills associated with leading, managing, and following should we
  focus on and develop?
• How well do we understand, empathize, and connect with people at all levels in the
  business to forge trusting relationships?
• What can we build into our way of working that allows us to foster trust and positive
  rapport with each other?

**Self-Awareness Lens:**

• As leaders, are we able to ask for help?
• Do we give and receive useful feedback in a constructive manner?
• Can we admit when we have made a mistake, yet not lose confidence?
• Do we "look in the mirror" frequently enough to understand our own personality,
  traits, strengths, and shortcomings and how these influence our interactions with others?

**Figure 8.1    Shockproof Lens Questions**

You have kept a running list of your key findings. The good news is that leaders have identified many areas in the business as operating effectively. That's good, but less important for your immediate task. You scan your notes for items that might make it on the short list for the offsite agenda. You focus on the most common areas of concern that were raised during the interviews:

- Lack of agreement on which markets to pursue and how to gain competitive advantage.

- Fear that any change in strategic direction would upset the balance of power or cause a shift in priorities and investments.

- Incomplete data gathering and analysis to identify future talent needs.

- Difficulty introducing new products because of poor collaboration across functions.

- Board concern over decisions that sacrifice long-term value for short-term gains.

- Too much focus on financial performance; not enough on customers.

- Lack of clarity around who owns what decisions at the midmanagement level.

- Duplication of effort by sales and marketing. Both are gathering customer insights with no coordination.

- A culture that tolerates mediocre performance.

- Laissez-faire senior leadership in an environment where many people are in new roles and need more guidance to build their capabilities and confidence.

Whew! You take a deep breath. It seems like a lot to tackle. You could easily add to this list based on your own observations, but you hold off. The list appears to include issues that relate to strategy, organization, talent, and leadership. The theme about laissez-faire leadership will be "fun," or at least interesting, to discuss at the offsite. You start to think through how the executive team can best be engaged to work with this list. You capture what you need to do to get ready.

## Prep Work for the Executive Offsite

1. Work with the CEO to categorize and simplify the interview findings and develop the offsite agenda.

2. Develop a simple *value tree* to illustrate the linkages between strategic objectives and the capabilities and processes that need to be in place to execute.

3. Send along a *short article* about the value of aligning strategy, organization, and *talent*, to improve strategy execution and business results.

4. Clean up and circulate the draft agenda below from your notes:

> *Shockproof Offsite*
> *Day One Outline*
>
> *CEO Overview: 60 minutes/1 hour*
>
> - *Current "state of the union" in our business.*
>
> - *Our current strategy and areas of focus based on last year's three-year view.*
>
> *Highlights of Interview Findings: 120 minutes/2 hours*
>
> - *Areas we need to address by category (strategy, organization, talent, and leadership).*
>
> - *Prioritize the most critical issues.*

*Strategy Clarification and Confirmation of Priorities*: 240 minutes/4 hours

- How do we intend to win against the competition?

- Review the value tree and discuss the capabilities, processes, and activities that add the most value.

- What is our current level of effectiveness in the areas that we believe are most important to execute the strategy?

- What should be our most immediate focus to improve strategy execution?

### Day Two Outline

*Organization Design Issues*: 120 minutes/2 hours

- How can we remove duplication of effort?

- Can we speed up decision making around new product introductions by clarifying who "has the call" and who owns key decisions at each step?

- How can we put a more balanced set of performance metrics in place?

- Review governance concerns raised by the board: Do we have the right "guardrails" in place to guide decisions and manage risk?

*Talent*: 120 minutes/2 hours

- Review recent talent segmentation initiative results: Do we agree on the roles that were categorized as strategic, core, and requisite?

- Talent gaps (midmanagement) and above based on recent succession planning.

- Why do we struggle to hire the type of talent we target?

*Leadership: 120 minutes/2 hours*

- *What can we do as leaders to create and sustain tighter connections between strategy, organization, and talent?*

- *Why are we failing to effectively mentor new talent?*

- *Which Shockproof Lenses do we each need to develop?*

*Next Steps and Wrap-up: 60 minutes/1 hour*

- *Develop commitment charts for each issue:*

  - *Who is the decision maker around how the issue will be resolved?*

  - *Who is recommending ideas and solutions?*

  - *Who has input into the recommendation?*

  - *Who has veto rights, if anyone (Legal? HR? Safety? Risk Management? Board?)*

  - *Who will be responsible for implementing the solution?*

While you are working on the agenda, you get a call from an old friend who tells you that he is frustrated with his company's performance. "No bonuses three years in a row, no resources to support 'important' priorities, a lot of dissatisfaction," he complains. You tell him about what you have been working on over the last few weeks and he listens with interest. As you continue to listen to his litany of complaints about what is not working at his company, you start to see some parallels between your business and his, and you offer to share what you have been up to and point him in the right direction.

"How do I get started," he asks?

You think a minute, and then offer the following advice: "I'd suggest to your manager that your group could benefit from getting aligned around the most important priorities that influence strategy execution. I'd tell him that you see a lot of fragmented focus, and that people seem to be spinning their wheels. You should be ready to share how this misalignment dilutes productivity, performance, and results; that will help to get his attention. You might offer to do a little research on what companies that weather the tough times and grab a hold of opportunities seem to have in common."

You also add, "Simple as it seems, this work is about getting the right people in a room to discuss what's happening in the business and to begin seeing things in a more integrated, holistic fashion. It is called being Shockproof, and a lot of companies are paying attention to how to develop this . . ."

Your friend interrupts you. "Whoa . . . I'm already there," he tells you. "I started Googling 'companies that weather the tough times' as soon as you started talking and the word *Shockproof* popped up all over my screen. So this is what has kept you so busy the last few weeks. Interesting. Looks like I have some reading to do."

With that, you say good-bye to each other. You send the draft agenda to your CEO and set up a time for the two of you to chat. As you get ready to shut down your touchscreen so you can go work out at the gym, you hear a swooshy sound and look back at the screen. There isn't anything there but the usual icons, but for a moment you thought you heard a big blue catfish darting away, swimming for cover.

# Notes

## Chapter 1

1. Mario Batali, "Bad Boys in the Kitchen: Gourmet Institute Weekend," *Gourmet*, October 23, 2004.

2. Jerry Butler, "Only the Strong Survive: The Iceman Cometh," Mercury Records, 1968.

3. Jim Collins, *Good to Great* (New York: HarperBusiness, 2001).

4. Ed Michaels, Helen Handfield-Jones, and Beth Axelrod, *The War for Talent* (Boston: Harvard Business Press, 2001).

5. Jim Collins, *Good to Great*, 13.

6. Tamar Elkeles, interview with Deb Jacobs, May 12, 2010.

7. Dan Sullivan, interview with Deb Jacobs, June 9, 2010.

## Chapter 2

1. *Life*, May 7, 1965.

2. Tara Kelly, "Can Crocs Be More Than a One-Hit Wonder," *Time*, October 9, 2009.

3. Mark Parker, Nike 2010 Investor Meeting, New York, NY, May 5, 2010.

4. Crocs, "Crocs, Inc. Reports 2010 First Quarter Financial Results," press release, May 6, 2010.

5. Norma Nieto, Keith Strange, and William Takis, "Strategic Responses to Recession: A Comparison of the U.S. Postal Service to Other Leading Companies." Paper presented at the 18th Conference on Postal and Delivery Economics by the Center for Research in Regulated Industries of Rutgers Business School, Porvoo, Finland, June 2–5, 2010.

6. Fred Smith, Message to Shareowners, FedEx Corporation, 2009 Annual Report.

7. Fred Smith, Interview with Academy of Achievement, May 23, 1998.

8. AccountingWeb, "BearingPoint: The End of an Era," July 29, 2009, www.accountingweb.com/topic/firm-news/bearingpoint-end-era.

9. Breck T. Marshall, interview with Juan Pablo González, May 3, 2010.

10. Edward T. Meehan, interview with Juan Pablo González, May 3, 2010.

11. Clayton M. Christensen, *The Innovator's Dilemma* (New York: Harper Paperbacks, 2003).

12. George H. Glatfelter II, Letter to Shareholders, P.H. Glatfelter Company, 2009 Annual Report.

13. *International Directory of Company Histories*, Vol. 30 (Farmington Hills, MI: St. James Press, 2000).

14. William T. Yanavitch II, interview with Juan Pablo González, April 7, 2010.

# CHAPTER 3

1. IBM, "IBM Agrees to Acquire Sterling Commerce from AT&T for $1.4 Billion," press release, May 24, 2010.

2. Sam Palmisano, IBM 2010 Annual Meeting of Stockholders, Milwaukee, WI, April 27, 2010.

3. Bob Irwin, interview with Garrett Sheridan, April 5, 2010.

4. Tim Wiggins, interview with Garrett Sheridan, April 29, 2010.

5. Edgar Huber, interview with Deb Jacobs, June 23, 2010.

6. Harry Kraemer, interview with Garrett Sheridan, May 10, 2010.

7. Wendell Weeks, Corning Incorporated 2010 Annual Shareholders Meeting, Corning, NY, April 29, 2010.

8. Abbie Liebman, "Corning Stories—Gorilla Glass," Corning, NY, June 2010, www.corning.com/news_center/corning_stories/gorilla_glass.aspx.

9. Curt Weinstein, interview with Garrett Sheridan, May 6, 2010.

10. Virginia Gambale, interview with Garrett Sheridan, May 18, 2010.

11. "JetBlue: Highest in Customer Satisfaction Among Low-Cost Carriers in North America," J.D. Power and Associates, 2010.

12. Clayton Christensen, "Where Dell Went Wrong," *BusinessWeek*, February 19, 2007.

13. Michael Dell, Sanford C. Bernstein & Company Strategic Decisions Conference, New York, NY, June 3, 2010.

## CHAPTER 4

1. "15 Biggest Job Losers," *Fortune*, May 13, 2010, http://money.cnn.com/galleries/2010/fortune/1005/gallery.fortune500_big_job_losses.fortune/index.html.

2. Bob Irwin, interview with Garrett Sheridan, April 5, 2010.

3. Tim Wiggins, interview with Garrett Sheridan, April 29, 2010.

4. David Hanna, *Designing Organizations for High Performance* (Reading, MA: Addison-Wesley, 1988.)

5. Marcia W. Blenko, Michael C. Mankins, and Paul Rogers, "The Decision-Driven Organization," *Harvard Business Review*, June 2010.

6. Refers to the drop in BP p.l.c.'s market capitalization from January 1, 2010, to June 25, 2010, following the explosion and subsequent oil spill of the Deepwater Horizon oil rig on April 20, 2010, in the Gulf of Mexico.

7. Mark Allan, interview with Garrett Sheridan, April 14, 2010.

8. John Tonkiss, interview with Garrett Sheridan, April 14, 2010.

9. Jesse Cates, interview with Garrett Sheridan, March 31, 2010.

10. Jim McNulty, interview with Garrett Sheridan, June 10, 2010.

11. Tom Moran, interview with Garrett Sheridan, April 12, 2010.

## CHAPTER 5

1. Scott Adams, *The Dilbert Principle* (New York: Harper Paperbacks, 1997).

2. Jack Welch, 2006 Banking Leaders Forum and Annual Convention, American Bankers Association, Phoenix, AZ, October 15–18, 2006.

3. Michael Lewis, *Moneyball: The Art of Winning an Unfair Game* (New York: W.W. Norton & Company, 2004).

4. Neustar History, Neustar Incorporated, www.foretec.com/about-neustar/about-tabs/history.

5. Doug Arnold, interview with Juan Pablo González, April 9, 2010.

6. John Adams, interview with Juan Pablo González, April 19, 2010.

7. Mike Hughes, interview with Juan Pablo González, April 19, 2010.

8. Larry Clifton, interview with Juan Pablo González, April 12, 2010.

9. Frank Maness, interview with Dave Kuhlman and Mark Masson of Axiom Consulting Partners, April 14, 2010.

10. Diane Brady, "Can GE Still Manage?" *BusinessWeek*, April 15, 2010.

11. Bob Eady, interview with Juan Pablo González, April 21, 2010.

12. Howard Walseman, interview with Juan Pablo González, April 21, 2010.

13. "The 50 Most Influential Minority Lawyers in America," *National Law Journal*, June 2, 2008.

14. Tracy Noon, interview with Garrett Sheridan and Juan Pablo González, May 12, 2010.

15. "T-Mobile: Highest Ranked Wireless Customer Service Performance," J.D. Power and Associates, 2009.

16. Bruce O'Neel, interview with Juan Pablo González, May 12, 2010.

17. Louis Montgomery, interview with Juan Pablo González, March 24, 2010.

18. Marc Effron and Miriam Ort, *One Page Talent Management: Eliminating Complexity, Adding Value* (Boston: Harvard Business Press, 2010).

19. "Smashing the Clock: No Schedules, No Mandatory Meetings. Inside Best Buy's Radical Reshaping of the Workplace," *BusinessWeek*, December 11, 2006.

20. Juan Pablo González, "Renewable Rewards for Renewable Enterprises," *workspan*, January 2010, 47–51.

# CHAPTER 6

1. Mark Allan, interview with Garrett Sheridan, April 14, 2010.

2. Bradley Keoun and Michael J. Moore, "Citi Loses $7.6 Billion on TARP Repayment," *BusinessWeek*, January 19, 2010, www .businessweek.com/bwdaily/dnflash/content/jan2010/db20100119 _283407.htm.

3. Joseph Plambeck, "10 Billionth Download for iTunes," *New York Times*, February, 25, 2010, Arts Section, www.nytimes .com/2010/02/26/arts/music/26arts-10BILLIONTHD_BRF .html.

4. "Speaking Out: Apple's and Pixair's Steve Jobs," *BusinessWeek*, August 25, 2003, www.businessweek.com/magazine/content/03_ 34/b3846633.htm.

5. Google Investor Relations, "2010 Financial Tables," Google, Inc., http://investor.google.com/financial/tables.html.

6. Jessica E. Vascellaro, Jason Dean, and Siobhan Gorman, "Google Warns of China Exit over Hacking," *Wall Street Journal*, January 13, 2010, Asia Technology Section, http://online.wsj.com/article/ SB126333757451026659.html.

7. Peter V. LeBlanc, "When the Business Zigs, Why Do the People Zag?" March 2006.

8. "15 Biggest Job Losers," *Fortune*, May 13, 2010, http://money .cnn.com/galleries/2010/fortune/1005/gallery.fortune500_big_ job_losses.fortune/3.html.

9. *Undercover Boss*, CBS, February 7, 2010.

10. Charles Fishman, "Face Time with Jeff Bezos," *Fast Company*, January 31, 2001, www.fastcompany.com/magazine/43/bezos.html.

11. Craig Harris, "In a Jolt, Starbucks Fires CEO, Replaces Him with Schultz," *Seattle PI*, January 7, 2008, Business Section, www .seattlepi.com/business/346397_sbuxdonald08.html.

12. Bruce Jacobson, interview with Garrett Sheridan, April 8, 2010.

13. Bill Hackett, interview with Garrett Sheridan, April 8, 2010.

14. John Carter, interview with Garrett Sheridan and Dave Kuhlman, April 23, 2010.

15. Bob Irwin, interview with Garrett Sheridan, April 5, 2010.

16. Jim Collins, *How The Mighty Fall: And Why Some Companies Never Give In* (New York: Jim Collins, an imprint of HarperCollins Publishers, 2009).

17. John Adams, interview with Juan Pablo González, April 19, 2010.

18. David Kirkpatrick and Tyler Maroney, "The Second Coming of Apple: Through a Magical Fusion of Man—Steve Jobs—and Company, Apple Is Becoming Itself Again: A Little Anticompany That Could," *Fortune*, November 9, 1998.

19. Betsey Morris, "Steve Jobs Speaks Out," *Fortune*, March 7, 2008, http://money.cnn.com/galleries/2008/fortune/0803/gallery.jobs-qna.fortune/7.html.

20. William J. Cook, "The Turnaround Artist," *U.S. News & World Report*, September, 6, 1996, www.usnews.com/usnews/biztech/articles/960617/archive_008990.htm.

21. Lou V. Gerstner Jr., MBA Distinguished Speaker Series, Georgetown University, McDonough School of Business, August 31, 2008.

22. Peter Woodman and Graeme Evans, "Ryanair Boss: Airline Industry Needs a Recession," *Independent*, November 3, 2008, www.independent.co.uk/travel/news-and-advice/ryanair-boss-airline-industry-needs-a-recession-988336.html.

23. Kevin Boyle, interview with Garrett Sheridan, June 18, 2010

24. Robert Sandall, "Off the Record," *Prospect*, August 1, 2007, www.prospectmagazine.co.uk/2007/08/offtherecord.

25. Claire Atkinson, "Sony Music Begins to Seek Schmidt-Holtz Successor," *New York Post*, July 15, 2010, www.nypost.com/p/news/business/auf_wiedersehen_HCPJR44x56Do2ClbLQDKnI.

# Chapter 7

1. Jerry Wenker, interview with Deb Jacobs, June 3, 2010.

2. Herb Greenberg, "How Doing the Right Thing Pays Off," *MarketWatch*, October 28, 2007, www.marketwatch.com/story/how-doing-the-right-thing-pays-off.

3. John P. Kotter, "Leading Change: Why Transformation Efforts Fail," *Harvard Business Review*, January 2007.

4. Edgar Huber, interview with Deb Jacobs, June 23, 2010.

5. Bob Irwin, interview with Garrett Sheridan, April 5, 2010.

6. Lisa Ricciardi, interview with Deb Jacobs, June 1, 2010.

7. Harry Kraemer, interview with Garrett Sheridan, May 10, 2010.

8. Michael Fleming, interview with Deb Jacobs, June 28, 2010.

9. Banner Health and Subsidiaries Consolidated Financial Statements Years Ended December 31, 2009, and 2008, April 9, 2010.

10. "Students Hear What It Takes to Be a CEO from Heads of Urban Outfitters and PRI," *ChicagoBooth News*, May 25, 2010, www.chicagobooth.edu/news/2010-05-25-road-to-ceo.aspx.

11. Bill Hackett, interview with Garrett Sheridan, April 8, 2010.

12. Len Lauer, interview with Deb Jacobs, May 10, 2010.

13. David Cunningham, interview with Deb Jacobs, May 14, 2010.

14. "Axiom Consulting Partners Strategy Execution Study: Survey Findings July 2009," Axiom Consulting Partners, July 2009, p. 28.

# ACKNOWLEDGMENTS

First, an enormous thank-you to the incredible business leaders whose accomplishments and perspectives are the fabric of *Shockproof*. We appreciate you for taking the time to share with us your stories and beliefs, and for letting us weave together your lessons so that we and our readers could learn from your successes. You are: John Adams (The Martin Agency), Mark Allan (UNITE), Doug Arnold (Neustar), Mila Baker (The World Bank), Joe Bonito (Bank of America), Kevin Boyle (Boyle & Associates), John Carter (PwC), Jesse Cates (Corning Incorporated), Kathy Chalmers (Sony Music), Larry Clifton (CACI), David Cunningham (Calvin Klein), Susan DiDonato (CommonHealth), Rad Eanes (ECCO), Bob Eady (American Bankers Association), Tamar Elkeles (Qualcomm), Becky Finger (Plato's Closet), Kate Finger (Plato's Closet), Dr. Michael Fleming (Banner Health), Virginia Gambale (JetBlue), Matt Giegerich (Ogilvy CommonHealth), Bill Hackett (Crown Imports LLC), Mark Henderson (Time Warner), Edgar Huber (Juicy Couture), Bob Irwin (Sterling Commerce), Mike Hughes (The Martin Agency), Bruce Jacobson (Crown Imports LLC), Harry Kraemer (Madison Dearborn Partners), Frank Maness (Novartis), Leslie Margolin (Anthem Blue Cross of California), Breck Marshall (Accenture), Ed Meehan (Accenture), Len Lauer (Memjet), Bill McComb (Liz Claiborne), Jim McNulty (NYSE), Louis Montgomery (Serco), Stephen Mooney (Tenet Healthcare), Tom Moran (Heidrick & Struggles), Tracy Noon (Hudson), Bruce O'Neel (T-Mobile), Michael Parisi (Altum), Lisa Ricciardi (Pfizer), Lawrence Sauder (Elswood-Sauder Industries), Ed Savage (L-3 Communications), Len Stephens (LEAP Cricket Wireless), Dan Sullivan (Qualcomm), Betty Thompson

(Booz Allen Hamilton), John Tonkiss (UNITE), Howard Walseman (American Bankers Association), Curt Weinstein (Corning Incorporated), Jerry Wenker (Dermalogica), Tim Wiggins (Tellabs), Bill Yanavitch (Glatfelter).

Of course, the Shockproof story also belongs to our colleagues at Axiom Consulting Partners, who build Shockproof organizations every day through the way they think about, help shape, and improve businesses. Your contributions are evident throughout this book. Thanks to John Anderson, Colleen Cahill, Donncha Carroll, Dave Danesh, Paul Dinan, Karen Jansen, David Kuhlman, Julie Maskulka, Mark Masson, Traci McCready, Susan Mlot, Kate Richardson, Don Ruse, Anna Sobieski, Aaron Sorensen, Steve Strelsin, Shannon Sullivan, and Sameer Tejani. Special thanks go to Axiom's Marketing Director, John Whelan, who early on convinced us that the world was ready to hear our message. He brought the idea to life and tended to it over the two years it took to develop it into the book you are reading today.

Our book would not have been possible without the talent and know-how the pros brought to our venture. We are especially grateful to Bill Gladstone, our agent, who believed in the Shockproof story early on and guided us to the phenomenal Shannon Vargo, Lauren Freestone, Peter Knox, and Elana Schulman at John Wiley & Sons, Inc. Along the way, Bill Hamby helped make the writing fun. His coaching taught us to trust that a book must have a unified voice before it can be given legs. Larry Hamby gets our accolades, as well, for tipping up his glass of wine one night and using his creative director capabilities to conceive the *Shockproof* title.

To all of those who have given us advice or lent an ear over the years: Steve Potter (Allyon Solutions), for his visionary belief in Axiom and his support of everything *Shockproof.*

Jean Christofferson and Ryan Johnson, from WorldatWork, who have helped us share our point of view with leaders around the world; Marc Effron, founder of the Talent Strategy Group, who has provided valuable counsel throughout this project; Jack Gocke, Ted Cadmus, Corey Anderson (Wells Fargo), Craig Stevens (Cabot Consultants), Jason Branciforte (Littler Mendelson P.C.), and Hector Velez (HireStrategy), who have unfailing supported our efforts to tell this story; and Ed Yingling and Ginney Dean (American Bankers Association), Christina Davis (Blind Industries and Services of Maryland), Bill Steele (T-Mobile), Michael Ronan (Starbucks), Kamilah Mitchell (Sony Music Entertainment), and Shane Spiers (UNITE), who have helped us round out our perspective. Susan Annunzio, Kevin Boyle, and Matthew Levin, who generously provided their support and perspective and connected us with like-minded leaders. Father Jason Brooks for his perspective on the importance of leadership, character, and values in today's business environment. Kittie Watson (CEO, Innolect, Inc.), for her unshakable belief in the wisdom and insight that only active listening can bring to leaders; Becky Ripley (Ripley Group), for modeling how graciousness and tenacity build positive legacy; Cindy Erickson, Michelle Sterling, and Pam Gibbes Smith, for living the principles that epitomize Shockproof thinking; and Carol Anderson (Carol E. Anderson & Associates Consulting) and Peter Norlin (Organization Development Network), for encouraging real dialogue and mastery.

Of utmost importance is our deep appreciation to our families, who endured phone calls at dawn, interrupted holidays, all-night write-a-thons, and seemingly endless days of interviews and editing—thank you for taking on more than your share so we could write this book about what makes businesses better.

# INDEX

Success, as an obstacle, 34
Successful change, implementing, 46
Sullivan, Dan, 19
Sun Microsystems, 149
Survival of the fittest, 4
Sustainability, 9
Sustainable organization, 38
Systemic thinking, 206
Systems Lens, 14, 45, 58, 89, 116, 129, 143,
        204–210, 236
    example of, 206–210
    focal points of, 205–206
    on JetBlue, 73
    valuing, 210
Systems Lens Showcase, 206–210

"Table stakes," 151
Takis, William, 28
Talent
    building, 110
    building versus buying, 122
    clear vision of, 123
    as an element of Shockproofing, 10, 12–13
    hiring, 173
    importance of, 111–112
    making the most of, 152
    managing, 35
    rewarding, 115–116
    segmenting, 113–114
    Shockproof approach to, 112–115
    during the tech boom, 111
    valuing, 109
Talent acquisition, 43, 112–113, 117–123
    effective, 121
    role in Shockproofing, 119
Talent analysis, 112
Talent deployment, 113–114, 123–131
    as a strategic advantage, 130–131
Talent development, 114–115, 131–138
    commitment to, 133–134
    hardwiring to strategy, 136
Talent intimacy, 227
Talent management, 12–13, 124–125
    Qualcomm, 17
    Shockproof approaches to, 117
Talent management practices, new,
        147–148
Talent pools, 18
Talent questions, 249
Talent segmentation, 127
Task, determining the size of, 93
Taylor, William, 136
Team member interests, 44
Teams, importance of, 196–197
Teamwork, 236

Technology
    importance of, 72–74
    investing in, 73–74
    leveraging, 98
Technology strategy, 72, 74
Tellabs Inc., 54–55, 81, 82–83
Thompson, Betty, 34–36
Time, 23
Time Warner, 80
T-Mobile, 141–142
    rewards at, 146, 148, 150–151
Tonkiss, John, 90, 91, 92, 102
Trading up, 96–98
Transactional work, reducing, 94–95
Transformational leaders, 13
Trust, inspiring, 225
Turner, Fred, 167
"Tyranny of the urgent," 46

United States Postal Service (USPS)
    decline of, 23, 28–30
    future of, 47
UNITE Group Plc, 88–92, 100, 102, 103, 105
    preparing for challenging times, 156–157
    transformation at, 90
UNITE leadership, 91–92
UNITE UK Student Accommodation Fund
        (USAF), 90
Unwinding, in organization design, 99–100
Up in the Air, 79

Value
    creating, 14, 15, 89, 97–98
    drivers of, 211–212
    measures of, 85–86
    measuring, 212
    perspective on, 212–213
    from Shared Services, 94
Value drivers, 247
Value Lens, 14, 46, 57, 59, 90, 94, 124, 129,
        147, 235
    focal points of, 211–212
    prioritizing via, 210–211
Value Lens Showcase, 213–215
Value tree, 182, 252
    benefits of, 187
Value tree mapping process, 90
VIA, 165, 166
Volanakis, Peter, 65
von Moltke, Helmuth, 49

Wall Street Journal, 23
Walseman, Howard, 133–134, 135, 136
"War for talent," 115–116